AVIATION
PIONEERS

A Collection of U.S. Stamps

TABLE OF
CONTENTS

INTRODUCTION

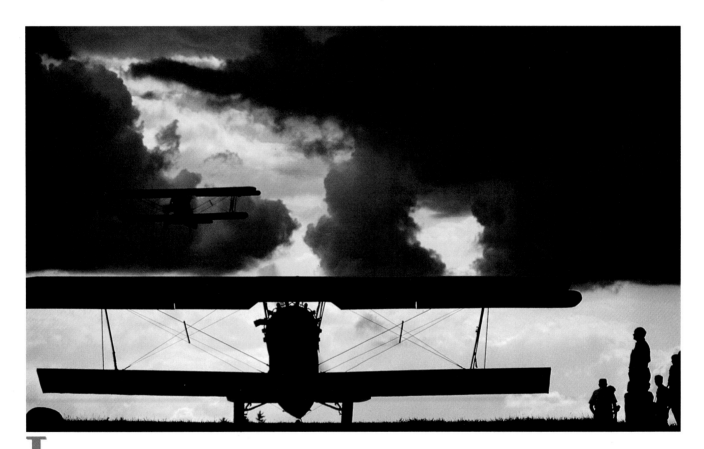

I guess it's no secret that I love flying and everything about it. But then, I'm hardly alone. The human race has been fascinated with aviation, and the *idea* of flying, ever since the beginning of recorded time.

Even today, in our modern, sophisticated world, I imagine that almost everyone who stops to watch an aircraft soar overhead is still captivated, for at least a brief instant, by the amazing reality of something so big and manmade actually being *up there*.

I even see that sense of wonder in the most jaded and bored of business travelers, when they stare out the window of a commercial jet, absorbed in the magical fact that they're really *flying*.

But aviation and all that it represents involves much more than a momentary sense of awe. Flight, and progress in flight, have been changing and improving human life since long before the Wright brothers first got their tiny plane to stay airborne for a few seconds just above the sand at Kitty Hawk.

Aviation has literally shrunk our world and expanded it at the same time, bringing nations closer together and enabling people to journey to and experience any place on earth.

I suppose it is inevitable that today, for many of us, flying is so routine and safe that we don't give it a second thought. But as you leaf through this fascinating book, I hope you'll reflect on the courage and conviction — and perhaps most importantly, the sheer spirit of adventure — that inspired the aviators and designers honored here.

I was born at just the right time to participate in what has been called the Golden Age of aviation. I had the fun of flying the early prop-driven fighters such as the P-39 and the P-51, and I got to pilot the P-51 in the ultimate type of flying: air-to-air combat. I also was privileged to be involved in the early days of jet aviation, most significantly breaking the sound barrier in the rocket-powered X-1, which opened the way into space flights.

Every generation has added some-

their beliefs by piloting their history-making airplane), there were no guarantees and seldom any ironclad formulas to ensure their safety aloft. In fact, both Quimby and Post died doing the thing they loved most — flying.

My hat is off to each of them. The romance of flying which they helped create and their daring deeds helped fuel my imagination as a youngster and buoyed my spirits as an adult when I was out there "on the edge of the envelope."

And as you read about their accomplishments, I think you'll experience the same wonderful sensation that flying, just the *thought* of flying, gave to those Aviation Pioneers and all who have come after them. ■

Chuck Yeager

While some veteran pilots like Chuck Yeager (far right) test the newest fighters, many beginners are enthralled by old biplanes (opposite) and newly built reproductions of ancient classics. One favorite is the Glenn Curtiss Headless Pusher of 1911, flying above.

thing to the advancement of flying. And today, technology seems to make it easy. But in contrast, the brave pioneers honored in this book were designing and flying on the proverbial wing and a prayer. The calculations of the Wrights, and Octave Chanute, and the Sperrys, and Igor Sikorsky, told them that their ideas and dreams *might* work. But outcomes were far from certain and they endured repeated risk and failure to achieve success.

Similarly, the brave pilots featured here often were soaring into the unknown. For pioneers like Glenn Curtiss, the trailblazing Harriet Quimby and Wiley Post (and don't forget the Wrights — they both backed

*I*n a field of stalwart individuals romanticized for their courage and daring as pilots, Brigadier General (USAF Ret.) Charles E. "Chuck" Yeager may represent the ultimate.

Test pilot extraordinaire, first man to fly faster than the speed of sound (in 1947) and more than twice the speed of sound (in 1953), Brig. Gen. Yeager was elected to the Aviation Hall of Fame in 1973; was awarded a peacetime Congressional Medal of Honor in 1976, and was presented the Presidential Medal of Freedom in 1985.

In addition to his nine-year assignment as the nation's leading test pilot, he flew some 183 types of aircraft during a distinguished 34-year military career that included shooting down 13 enemy aircraft during World War II — five on one mission — and escaping capture after being shot down himself over German-occupied France.

Among key postwar activities, the West Virginia native was Commandant of the Aerospace Research Pilot School, where all military astronauts are trained; flew 127 missions in South Vietnam while Commander of the 405th Fighter Wing, and served as Director of the Air Force Inspection and Safety Center.

In addition to a wealth of military decorations and awards, Brig. Gen. Yeager, who now resides in California, earned such aviation honors as the Mackay and Collier Trophies in 1948 and the Harmon International Trophy in 1954. ■

A U.S. airmail stamp issued in 1953 commemorated the golden anniversary of the Wright brothers' historic flight that ushered in aviation.

OCTAVE CHANUTE

I t's all so familiar. The crowded cabin, the bored voices with their ritual messages about seats, trays and seat belts, about no smoking, about being No. 3 to take off. Then at last there is the usual surge of power, pressing us back in our seats. And yet, when the rumble of the wheels stops and their vibration ends with a muffled thump, there are still many of us who glance out the window to see the ground dropping away and to feel again the old thrill of taking part in a miracle.

Human flight in a winged machine would certainly have required a miracle in the mid-19th century. It was as impossible as perpetual motion, and those who pursued the distant prospect of it were considered at best barely sane. So why in the world was a highly respected civil engineer such as Octave Chanute fooling around with this so-called science, this "aeronautics"? He was a builder of sensible things like railroads and bridges. Why did he waste himself and his time on the impossible prospect of human flight?

No one can be sure of the answer, but we can all be grateful that this brilliant and affable engineer with friends and admirers in high places had a secret obsession — an "affair" with a dream: human flight. As the dream neared reality, Chanute lent advice, judgment and publicity to every serious experiment in heavier-than-air aviation in Europe and the United States. He had the prestige, enthusiasm and generosity to raise aeronautics from the lowly sphere of the crackpot to the lofty realm of the engineer.

A brilliant engineer, Octave Chanute backed and encouraged early aviation.

Chanute is a French name, and one look at the short, stoutish man with the small white goatee under a white moustache provided convincing proof of his origins. He was born in Paris, and though his father took him to New Orleans at the age of six, he was kept carefully cloistered from the boisterous America of the 1840s.

Private tutoring kept his French tongue pure until, at age 11, he was prepared for an American school. All his life he had a certain "Frenchness" that added charm to his manner and a special liveliness to his talents.

Endlessly busy, highly successful— he built miles of railroads and the first bridge across the Missouri River — Chanute was once asked by a friend to name his hobby. He demurred, saying: "Wait until your children are not present, for they would laugh at me."

Though the notion of human flight was certainly laughable, it tugged at Chanute as early as 1866. Quietly, he followed the arcane developments of aeronautics and noted the papers read at various meetings of the true believers. One, by a curious Englishman named Francis Wenham, stirred him, Chanute wrote years later, with "an account of his own experiments with... aeroplanes of sufficient size to carry the weight of a man."

Wenham's description of his second plane especially intrigued Chanute. It had six thin, fabric "wings" mounted in a vertical row, to compress the job of lifting into a small, controllable space instead of spreading it over one huge, awkward surface. Wenham's multiplane didn't work because the fabric wasn't stiffened and simply fluttered in the wind. But, noted Chanute, "This principle is entirely sound."

When, 30 years later, Chanute had attained such eminence that he could admit to his eccentric interest and actually try out some gliders, he remembered Wenham's report and built one with a number of wings stacked atop each other. An awkward mass of wires and struts, it was dubbed *Katydid* by Chanute's assistants. Unfortunately, when it came to making a decent flight, *Katy* didn't. Its best glide was only around 80 feet.

This short attempt took place in 1895 over the sand dunes along Lake Michigan's Indiana shore. By this time, having made his pile in the highly competitive, big-money arena of railroading, Chanute was giving full time to his avocation.

Though too old to fly, Chanute poses amid the multiple wings of his glider, Katydid, *on Lake Michigan's shore. Pilots Avery (left) and Herring hold the wings. Fly well* Katy *didn't, until design was simplified to a biplane such as the Wright brothers later used.*

He'd gathered his reports of aviation experiments into a newly published book, *Progress in Flying Machines*, which had become a "must" for every would-be aviator. He'd also corresponded with the great Otto Lilienthal in Germany, whose glides from the round hills of Rhinow set impressive records before he was killed. Thanks to Chanute's publicizing these events, Lilienthal became a minor hero to Americans. A Boston newspaper reporter even tried out a Lilienthal hang glider and wrote that "sliding down the aerial incline" was "most delightful and wholly indescribable."

In Indiana, Chanute sought the same success with his gliders. At age 64 he was a bit too old to fly himself, but he dashed across the sand hills after the flights of younger men who shared his obsession, bursting with congratulations, with suggestions. With one young assistant, Augustus M. Herring, Chanute eventually reduced the number of *Katydid's* wings to two, tight and trim, making it a graceful biplane.

Issued:
March 29, 1979
Chanute, KS

"Being a builder of bridges," the engineer wrote, "I trussed these surfaces together in order to obtain strength and stiffness." He used a Pratt truss: vertical wooden spars to keep the wings apart, diagonal wire stays to hold them together.

Now both Herring and another assistant, William Avery, made splendid glides, skimming over the sand for well beyond 200 feet, even surpassing 350 feet on one occasion. Chanute's biplane was proved a successful concept, and seven years later the Wright brothers followed the design, with the same truss pattern, in the world's first powered and piloted airplane.

By then the Wrights had adopted the genial, hard-working Franco-American as a consultant, a sounding board for their ideas. Wilbur Wright

had written to him in May 1900, introducing himself as one "afflicted with the belief that flight is possible" and asking Chanute's help in tracking down aeronautical research. He received a quick answer, and a correspondence started that would fill a book. Wilbur and Orville were flattered by Chanute's interest, for by the turn of the 20th century, the engineer's interest in and understanding of aeronautics had become accepted, even by the unbelievers.

As a member of the Wrights' team, the famous old engineer was generally useful and invariably ebullient. He helped the brothers find the proper place to experiment. They needed plenty of steady breeze and soft sand to land on, and finally found it at Kitty Hawk on the secluded Outer Banks of North Carolina. He also helped them

Stable, well-engineered Chanute triplane glides off the sand dunes in 1897. Pilot (right) gets a good ride from a biplane, far less complex than Chanute multiplane of 1896 (top right), with its 11 (count 'em) lifting surfaces.

find materials for their experimental gliders. The brothers wanted spruce for their long wing spars. Spruce would be hard to find, said Chanute, and indeed, Wilbur had to settle for white pine.

As tests progressed, Chanute offered to pull strings with Andrew Carnegie so the Wrights could get a grant from the millionaire. They turned that down. Chanute advised them about patenting the new aeronautical gimmicks they were constantly developing. They postponed that decision, even though their friend hinted that the field was becoming crowded and competitive.

He told them what was going on among Europe's would-be flyers: Louis-Pierre Mouillard, who had a glider in France; Alberto Santos-Dumont, a transplanted Brazilian who had enthralled Paris by buzzing about the Eiffel Tower in a powered balloon and now wanted to build a plane; the members of aeronautical clubs and societies.

It seemed to the brothers that Chanute's concern with patents was unnecessary. They had already applied for one. They knew that the technicalities of their gliders owed nothing to the work of others, and they were puzzled that Chanute didn't see the differences as clearly as they did. Often his suggestions trespassed on their own carefully considered plans. They tried to maintain polite aloofness from him, but gradually he became their gadfly, visiting their primitive, sand-blown little camp at Kitty Hawk and badgering them with letters when they were intent on solving specific problems their own way.

Chanute was slow to understand how protective of their studies the Wrights were becoming. The brothers found his very enthusiasm threatening, for he was apt to sound off in a pamphlet or article with a premature report on their prospects of success. One misunderstanding led to another and the

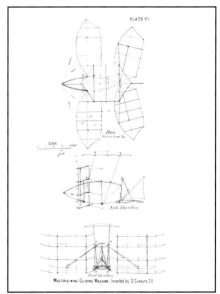

inventors' relationship cooled with their old friend and consultant.

The Wrights' first powered flights at Kitty Hawk, in 1903, slipped right over the head of the general public without notice. Not for five years were the brothers "discovered." Then their success aroused human imaginations in Europe and America, opening the gate to a new field of endeavor: aviation. It grew so fast that many an old-timer who had long awaited its birth couldn't keep pace with it.

Chanute had trouble keeping up, but he continued to write papers on his old obsession. He died in 1910 as flights grew longer, faster, more daring, yet safer. One pilot, Eugene Ely, even managed to land and take off from a naval vessel during this year.

Octave Chanute's place in the Air Age is secure. He was one of its godfathers. He was sometimes a pesky nuisance but always a bulwark of support. He occasionally offered misguided opinions but generally provided a reservoir of solid technical information. Unquestionably, he lent respectability to a field that had sadly lacked it, and his unfailing eagerness for the realization of human flight inspired those on the front line of invention.

Spare him an appreciative thought the next time you see the ground drop away beneath the wing of your 747. ■

SAMUEL P. LANGLEY

To some engineers and scientists, the prospect of human flight was like a bewitching siren. Octave Chanute gave in early, openly acknowledging his passion for this elusive temptress in 1886, at a meeting of the prestigious American Association for the Advancement of Science in Buffalo, New York. Chanute arranged for an amateur ornithologist, Israel Lancaster, to be included in the Buffalo program. He knew that Lancaster specialized in bird flight and the prospects of humans emulating it.

Lancaster's talk was a flop. The gathering of scientists hooted at this layman with his unproven assumptions.

But he did ignite a small blaze in the disciplined soul of Samuel Pierpont Langley, the distinguished astronomer. Before his inventive fire was doused, Langley would build the first successful heavier-than-air flying machine and would see the best of his pilotless creations stay aloft on a test run of some 4,200 feet in length.

Langley was what zoologists would call an alpha male: a dominant presence, big, bearded, handsome, with piercing eyes and total self-assurance. Though a devoted scholar of the highest caliber, he'd always felt a certain fascination for flight, and the meeting at Buffalo stirred this latent interest. Chanute had hoped the subject would snare a few fellow devotees. He didn't realize what a big catch it had hooked.

In the late 19th century it was not extraordinary for a person to achieve eminence without scrabbling after post-graduate degrees — without, in fact, even attending a university, Langley was an example. He was born in 1834 in Roxbury, Massachusetts, to a wealthy mercantile family. His schooling followed the path of the elite to Boston Latin. But after high school, he chose to veer away before it led to Harvard. He craved the real world and traveled to exuberantly youthful Chicago to find work in drafting and civil engineering.

Blessed with a bit of money and a restless mind, Langley taught himself astronomy, built a telescope, traveled abroad, and finally returned to Boston and went to Harvard after all — as an assistant at its observatory. The prestige of that post gained him the directorship of the U.S. Naval Academy Observatory in Annapolis, Maryland. He also taught math to the midshipmen.

This step into academe fitted him for the next: physics professor at the University of Pennsylvania in Pittsburgh and director of the Allegheny Observatory. Langley raised that observatory's reputation to new heights, exploring the mysteries of astrophysics, making important measurements of solar radiation, and earning coveted international scientific medals. The man who never went to college was awarded honorary degrees from Oxford, Cambridge, Harvard, Yale and Princeton.

More important to him than all these gratifying honors was his new obsession with flight. After the Buffalo meeting that triggered it, Langley returned to Pittsburgh, read everything in sight that dealt with aeronautics, and set up two 30-foot arms attached to a

rotating upright shaft. Soon the device was whirling dramatically at the Allegheny Observatory, testing how various plane surfaces passed through the air at 70 miles per hour.

When he first came to the Smithsonian Institution in 1887, as assistant secretary, the scientist returned frequently to his great whirling arms to measure the forces of lift and drag. But later, as secretary of the nation's unique scientific and educational institution, he was caught up in the whirl of Washington's social life, lionized by senators and cabinet members, and befriended by none other than Alexander Graham Bell — a fortuitous occurrence, for even the inventor of the telephone was now deeply interested in human flight.

Langley had begun experimenting with small model planes before he settled in Washington. As head of the Smithsonian, he had the use of staff carpenters to continue his design ideas. His 30 to 40 designs were no mere paper darts but were serious miniature

An imposing scientist, Samuel P. Langley was seduced from astronomy to aviation and, while heading the Smithsonian, tested a series of flying models. Workers (opposite) assemble his Great Aerodrome on its Potomac River barge.

aircraft — biplanes, monoplanes, tandem-winged planes — a yard or so from nose to tail, made of wooden spars with paper-covered wings and one or two

Issued:
May 14, 1988
San Diego, CA

propellers, spun by twisted rubber bands, to push or pull.

Langley rebuilt them several times, altering their designs, but didn't learn as much from them as he'd hoped. They needed more power. Steam engines would be better. So in the '90s, he began building models large enough to carry small, lightweight steam engines. He recruited gifted staff members and set them to work in their various shops and in a shed on Smithsonian grounds.

In the spring of 1892, his first steam-powered aircraft was born: No. 0. He called it an "aerodrome." The name came from the Greek *aerodromoi* ("air runner"). He felt it sounded better, even though it doesn't mean the same thing.

No. 0 was too heavy and too flimsy for its nice little engine with coppercoil boiler. He got his crew going on No. 1, then No. 2 and No. 3 — this last to be powered by a carbon dioxide engine. He also figured out a catapult to launch these big, relatively heavy aerodromes and bought a shallow-draft barge with a shack on board where the device could be rigged. This would allow test flights over the Potomac River, where the aerodromes could land without damage.

Gradually, the models got better. No. 4, steam-powered again, was good enough to try from the "Scow." But the lightest breeze tended to buckle the wings. It was rebuilt. No. 5 appeared and, late in 1894, managed to climb up and away from the Scow momentarily before stalling out.

Langley's greatest moments came in 1896. In the spring, aerodrome No. 4 — now so thoroughly redesigned that it became No. 6 — flew faultlessly for more than half a mile. No. 5 did almost as well. In awe, Alexander Graham Bell watched the flights of these beautifully crafted little planes with wingspans of more than 12 feet.

"For the first trial," Bell wrote, "the apparatus, chiefly constructed of steel...advanced against the wind, and while drifting little and slowly ascending, it described a curve of about one hundred metres in diameter and having been driven in its course for about a minute and a half...at a height in the air which I estimate at 81 feet, the revolutions of the screws ceased, for want of steam...."

In late fall of 1892, No. 6 flew 4,200 feet, holding a steady course, "about eight or ten yards above the water." Langley indeed had built the first successful heavier-than-air flying machine.

But it couldn't carry a pilot. The renowned professor, fully aware of his stature in the world of science, decided to go for the big prize — the world's first man-carrying airplane. Thanks to his prestige and influential friends like Bell and Chanute, he found funds — mostly from the government. The Spanish-American War, recently over, had given the Army ideas about flying.

To Langley, the project seemed almost simple: expand the aerodrome design to carry a wing surface of some 1,200 square feet. He did not consider the need for a quantum leap in structural strength.

By 1903 the Great Aerodrome was nearly ready. It was beautifully built — the professor's demand for perfection saw to that — and it was powered by a beautiful gasoline engine, a radial, one of the world's first. It could put out 52 horsepower. Langley had acquired the perfect assistant, Charles M. Manly of Virginia. Bright, gutsy, loyal to his boss

yet unafraid of him, Manly took over the building of the engine. He also agreed to pilot the Great Aerodrome.

A formidable prospect! Lacking landing gear, Manly would be catapulted off a new, bigger houseboat, then have to ditch in the Potomac. If he drifted over shore, he'd have to crashland. There was no way to bank and turn. Nevertheless Manly was in the "car," on October 8, 1903, with a compass sewed on one trouser leg. His engine sounded good. The press and notable onlookers were on hand. This was the great moment.

"I gave the order to release the car," noted Manly. He sped the length of the catapult but instead of being automatically released, "experienced a slight jerk and discovered immediately that the machine was plunging forward and downward...."

Poised on its catapult in October 1903, Aerodrome, with pilot Charles Manly aboard, revs up for a place in history.

After two tries and two failures (left), a shattered Langley retired from the race to fly first. His studies had included minute examinations of bird feathers (above) but insufficient testing of his full-sized plane. A wind tunnel would have revealed its weaknesses.

Into the water went the Great Aerodrome, "like a handful of mortar," in the words of a reporter. Manly got out without injury and without having to refer to his compass.

A fouled-up release mechanism was blamed for the crash. But photographs reveal the front wing buckling while the plane was still on the catapult. The structure itself failed.

Two months later, repaired and renewed, the big would-be bird was back on its catapult track for another try. Langley knew that a couple of unknown brothers from Ohio were fooling around with some sort of machine on the Outer Banks of North Carolina. Chanute said they were going to make it. Langley's whole reputation depended on beating them into the air.

December 8, 1903, was a gray, gusty day, quickly darkening by 4 p.m. Despite poor conditions, Langley and Manly agreed to give the flight a try. It would be months before the weather would allow another chance.

Manly eyed the ice-clogged river, then stripped to his BVDs and wriggled into a cork life jacket. He mounted to

the cockpit, listened to the blast of his lovely little engine, then signaled for his release. The Great Aerodrome shot forward, then the pilot "felt an extreme swaying motion immediately followed by a tremendous jerk which caused the machine to quiver all over."

Wires parted, fittings snapped, and wings crumpled as the nose rose

Great Aerodrome was simply an expanded version of the tandem-winged models Langley had flown successfully. He had never tried a man-carrying glider.

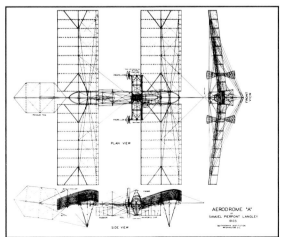

straight up and over. Manly hung from his inverted "car," entering the icy water feet first. The plane, breaking up, fell over him like a great canopy. Desperately, he tore off the life jacket and dove through the tangled guy wires. Lungs bursting, he rose and found he was under ice. Diving again, he managed to swim clear and finally surface — in time to see one of the crew dive in after him.

When he was finally hauled aboard the barge, the nearly frozen pilot was wrapped in a blanket and given a shot or two of whiskey, which produced a "voluble series of blasphemies." An understandable reaction.

The press, the government, the public reacted, too, scoffing at Langley, decrying the whole idea of flight. The only thing Langley had made fly, charged one congressman, "was government money." Another questioned the final price of flying, considering that it had "cost us $73,000 to construct a mud duck that will not fly over 50 feet."

Numbed by disappointment and embittered by public opinion, Samuel Langley shouldered his disgrace, forfeited his old dream, and vanished from the scene. Only nine days later, those unknown brothers from Ohio would succeed where he had failed. ■

ORVILLE & WILBUR WRIGHT

T he flat crackle of a distant gasoline engine is a strange sound on the Outer Banks of North Carolina in 1903.

But for the last few days, men of the U.S. Lifesaving Service at Kill Devil Hill have grown accustomed to it. It comes from that two-winged machine that the brothers from Ohio have built at their camp across the dunes, and on this bitter December morning it means that they're going to run that thing down its 60-foot rail and maybe hop it across a stretch of blowing sand. Gusts of cold wind pick up the sound and toss it about, so that to the watchers it undulates, loud, then faint, then loud again.

Some of the lifesavers watch the machine. Others have walked across to the brothers' camp, for this morning they flew the little flag that means they could use some help. Crazy or not, everyone likes them.

They're honest and friendly and mind their own business, and everyone hopes they won't break their fool necks.

The little engine still hammers away, warming up. But now the brothers walk a short distance from it, the wind snapping and tugging at their dark suits and neckties. They shake hands. One viewer will remember, 20 years later, that they "held on to each other's hand, sort o' like two folks parting who weren't sure they'd ever see one another again."

Now one turns back and clambers onto the lower wing of the machine, lying prone beside the rattling engine. The other holds on to a wing tip and stares out over the sand into history....

They were the third and fourth sons of Bishop Milton Wright, a noted mover and shaker of the United Brethren Church. A bright, energetic man with strong principles, Wright had chosen unusual names for his sons: first Reuchlin, then Lorin (named for a town), then Wilbur, and four years later, Orville. Little Katharine (with two "a"s) came last. Bright, attractive kids all of them, and closely knit as Victorian families were. After the two older boys grew up and moved on, Wilbur became the leader. An astute, poised young man, he was aimed for Yale when complications from a hockey injury sidelined him.

Orville, bright, creative and mechanical, had no intention of continuing school longer than he had to. He wanted to learn printing and built a press, with the help of Wilbur and their father, out of junk parts — including a piece of tombstone. Then he talked Will into helping put out a surprisingly successful neighborhood newspaper.

After their mother's death, Will, Orv and Katharine stayed on, taking care of the Bishop, maintaining home and family. Katharine went off to Oberlin, the only one of the young Wrights to go to college. In 1892, as the bicycle fad swept America, the two boys set up a repair shop and soon were building their own models. When they badly needed a particular tool — an electric welder, a gas engine to run their machine tools — they simply made it. That was the way they were.

Their interest in human flight began when Wilbur read of the death of the German, Otto Lilienthal, in a hang glider. What had this brave, ingenious man been trying to do? Wilbur's first letter to the Smithsonian Institution, seeking information about man's attempts to fly, is written in the first person, indicating that the interest, in 1899, wasn't fully shared by Orville. Will was 32 and craved a commitment. When he found it, poring through the books and pamphlets that the Smithsonian sent or suggested, Orv joined him as full partner.

The Wrights studied flight without preconceived ideas and decided that any flying machine must be fully controlled by its pilot. A radical idea! Octave Chanute and Lilienthal had considered control a matter of shifting weight in an inherently stable aircraft. Samuel Langley built impressive stability into his aerodromes by setting the wings considerably less than parallel — from a front view, they had the shape of a flattened "V."

Even Langley's full-sized version was designed to fly without rolling from side to side. All his assistant Charles Manly was supposed to do was raise or lower the nose and fiddle with the engine. Expert Tom Crouch of the Smithsonian, whose books *A Dream of Wings* and *The Bishop's Boys* are must reading for aviation buffs, says that Langley's Great Aerodrome was simply "the world's largest model airplane."

But the Wrights had the athlete's knack of picturing motions before they made them: the roll of one's weight on a bicycle as it rounds a corner; similarly, the banking of an aircraft as it makes a turn. They knew they would need full control of roll, pitch and yaw.

Issued:
September 23, 1978
Dayton, OH

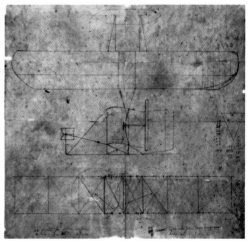

Striding toward destiny (left) the Wrights talked and argued endlessly about flight, drew up sketches like that above — on wrapping paper — of their 1903 plane, then tested theories in their wind tunnel and on the dunes. Orville snapped the 1902 glider (opposite) in tethered flight. Will holds the farther line.

Studying, corresponding steadily with Chanute, feeling out their own ideas, the brothers designed their first glider and assembled it in the fall of 1900 at Kitty Hawk on the lonely Outer Banks of North Carolina. It was little more than a kite but big enough to give Wilbur Wright his first ride on the bosom of the air.

In July 1901, they were back on the dunes of Kill Devil Hill and, while suffering agonies from mosquitoes, managed to build a simple hangar and finish their new glider, the largest ever flown up to that time. It had an elevator — a movable airfoil forward of the wings, to prevent the plane from stalling out — and it glided for considerable distances, teaching the Wrights a great deal. They fussed with the airfoil of the wings, the curve of the upper surface that gives lift. They tried out new, more efficient ways to launch and got glides well beyond 300 feet. Chanute, visiting them that August, was impressed.

Yet the brothers were concerned that some of the book lore they had studied seemed to be wrong. That winter they made the world's first air tunnel from a six-foot-long wooden box and tested the lift and drag of various airfoils. They gained a wealth of tested knowledge that refuted much of what previous experimenters had learned, and made their own success quite certain.

Their 1902 glider, built with the airfoil that had tested best, was larger than before, yet lighter. It had a vertical rudder in the rear and a hip cradle which the prone pilot could rock from side to side, thus tugging wires which altered the slant of the wings, warping them to make the plane bank.

Back at their beloved sand dunes that September, they made wonderful, controlled flights of 500 to 600 feet. They learned that their rudder should be able to turn, that it was needed as they banked. By the end of October, they knew that all they needed now was mechanical power. Then they would fly. They were perfectly sure of it.

Returning to Dayton, the young men went to work with their bicycle mechanic and built their own gasoline engine. It was crude, not in the same class as the beautifully made, powerful little radial that Manly had finished for Langley. But it met the Wrights' weight requirement — they'd wanted it no heavier than 150 pounds, and settled for 180 — and it well surpassed the eight horsepower they'd figured would get them into the air.

They decided to give the same attention to propeller design that they had to their wings, so they shaped the blade into a proper airfoil. The design was a marvel, entirely different from the scores of propellers that had been built and tried up to that time. The Wright propeller design is now recognized as one of their great breakthroughs. "Isn't it wonderful," wrote a pleased Orville to a friend, "that all these secrets have been preserved for so many years just so that we could discover them."

The pair worked feverishly to build the new, bigger biplane that would carry the engine and incorporate all the things they'd learned with the 1902 glider. In late September 1903, they arrived at their old camp on the Outer Banks, cleaned the hangar and repaired storm damage, then dusted off last year's glider and began flying it to see if they'd lost their touch.

They hadn't. By the time their shipments of crated engine and structural parts arrived, they'd made some

World's most famous photograph shows Orville's takeoff in the first plane as Wilbur watches. Epochal flights of December 17, 1903, rated only a brief description in Orville's telegram (right).

impressive glides and managed to soar without wavering, almost as if untouched by the ocean breeze.

In a letter to his sister, Wilbur noted that the "whopper flying machine" was being assembled and should be finished about November 1. That was three weeks after Langley's first attempt. After they learned of the Great Aerodrome's October disaster, Will wrote Chanute, "I see that Langley has had his fling, and failed. It seems to be our turn to throw now, and I wonder what our luck will be."

Bad weather slowed them down. Chanute arrived at camp and in the course of conversation asked the brothers if they'd demonstrate the old biplane glider that he and Augustus Herring had designed. Will and Orv realized that their famous friend still considered them merely expert glider pilots — not serious inventors on the verge of triumph. He seemed unaware of all they had done.

They tinkered with the engine, trying to increase its revolutions per minute. The specter of Langley preparing for his second attempt at powered flight hung over them.

Wilbur Wright, in the 1901 glider (right), checks out an airfoil, the curve of a wing surface which produces lift. The brothers found accepted figures on airfoil efficiency were wrong. They had to correct errors and, meanwhile, learn to fly — no one could teach them. They built a hangar and workshop at Kitty Hawk but had to repair them after winter storms. In the shop (below), Orville works on the wing of a glider.

They argued about details and improvements as they always did — noisily, yet without hard feelings. Their mechanic noted that he once heard them go at it fiercely one evening without a solution. Next morning each admitted he'd been wrong and the other was right, and "first thing I knew they were arguing the thing all over again, only this time they'd switched."

An engine test in late November revealed a cracked propeller shaft. Orville set off for Dayton. He was returning with new shafts on December 9 when he heard the news of Langley's final failure. Newspapers trumpeted about the insanity of manned flight.

On December 14, the weather was good, the new shafts in place. The Wrights flipped a coin. Will won and took his place. Men from the Lifesaving Station, who had often helped with the gliders, had been alerted and were there as witnesses as well as assistants.

With a great racket from the engine, the plane hummed down its rail, lifted, then soared up suddenly, stalled, and mushed back down to the sand. Wilbur, unhurt, realized that he'd raised the forward elevator too abruptly and too much. He'd done something a lot of new pilots have done ever since on their first flights. He'd overcontrolled.

There was little damage, and the Wrights quickly fixed it. By December 17 all was ready again, and though the weather was miserably cold and windy they knew they must go for it or wait until spring....

So the watchers see them shake hands, and now it's Orv's turn. He takes his place in the cradle on the wing, one hand on the elevator control, one on a lever that cuts off fuel to the engine and releases the line that holds the pioneering plane on the rail.

Will gets the ground crew organized — especially the man with a camera — then expectantly takes his position at the right wingtip.

The engine is warm. Orv moves the lever to release the plane. It rolls, then lifts and flies, bobbing up and down uncertainly as Orville, too, overcontrols. One dip ends in the sand and the first flight is over.

But the moment has occurred that the world has awaited. A human being has guided a machine into the air to fly some 120 feet and land — *uphill*, if anything, from where he started.

One lifesaver hurries back to the station to shout the news: "They done it! Damned if they ain't flew!" ■

GLENN CURTISS

The Wrights flew four times on December 17, 1903. They alternated at the controls, each improving on the other's flight, until Will stayed up for almost a minute and covered nearly 300 yards. They then packed up for Dayton in order to perfect, redesign and test.

The press paid little attention to their big day at Kitty Hawk. But three years later the first flights were given a little publicity by an article in *Scientific American*. One result was the brothers' first meeting with a bright, taciturn technician who had been designing superb lightweight engines to power bicycles.

Glenn Hammond Curtiss, named for Watkins Glen and Hammondsport in his native Finger Lakes country of upstate New York, wasn't unlike the Wrights. He was shy, thoughtful, energetic, about seven years younger than Orville. The Wrights, seemingly so similar in character, should have liked him from the start.

Instead, they wound up battling Curtiss for years through patent lawsuits and court injunctions before, ironically, teaming with him to form one of the world's largest aircraft corporations. And along the way Curtiss designed and flew planes which set many speed and distance records and earned him worldwide recognition.

Curtiss wasn't the motorbike's inventor. But until he began producing his Hercules "moto-cycles," the machines remained noisy, dangerous curiosities. His engines were light enough to race with and young Glenn, already a locally famous bike racer, began setting motorcycle speed records that would eventually earn him the title of the World's Fastest Man.

His machines caught the attention of "Captain" Tom Baldwin, a noted balloonist and circus man who saw the potential in aviation for light, powerful engines. Baldwin befriended the reticent young mechanical wizard and let him fly one of his powered, elliptical balloons — Glenn's first flight.

Thanks to Baldwin, Curtiss realized that the Wright brothers, who were rumored to have actually gotten off the ground, might be interested in his product. So he wrote them, and in the summer of 1906, when he was helping Captain Baldwin at a balloon show near Dayton, he dropped in. They chatted amiably, but the Wrights were more interested in improving their own engine than buying one from Curtiss.

Curtiss did better with Alexander Graham Bell. The great inventor was enthusiastically building man-carrying kites made of hundreds of tetrahedral-shaped cells. He thought a Curtiss engine might turn one of the kites into a genuine flying machine.

Bell invited Curtiss to his summertime estate, Beinn Breagh, near Baddeck, Nova Scotia, and the self-made, hardscrabble, grease-stained "speed merchant" and manufacturer was overwhelmed with the generous hospitality of the famous, white-bearded inventor, his wife and his friendly young assistants. They wanted him to join their Aerial Experiment Association (AEA) as "director of experiments."

The object of the AEA, in Bell's words, was "to get into the air." Money was no object. Mabel Bell would put up the sizable sum of $20,000 for starters, and her husband was offering salaries, with Curtiss to get the lion's share: $5,000 a year. Glenn couldn't say no.

Flying Bell's kite was No. 1 on the AEA's program. It was towed into the air with team member Tom Selfridge perched among the honeycombed cells. It rose with him to 168 feet, then landed so gently that Selfridge, with

Glenn H. Curtiss (left) built fast, handsome planes that set records. One, flown by Eugene Ely, first landed on and took off (above) from a ship. Famed stunt pilot Lincoln Beachey flew a Curtiss Pusher (opposite).

barely any visibility from among those cells, didn't realize he was down and allowed himself to be dragged through lake water until the structure fell apart.

Next project: build an airplane. Nova Scotia's harsh winter drove them to Curtiss' hometown, Hammondsport, where they planned to fly off the ice of Lake Keuka. The Alexander Bells moved in with Curtiss and his young wife, and the telephone's inventor caused chuckles by complaining that the thing rang too much.

Issued:
December 30, 1980
Hammondsport, NY

In March 1908, the Red Wing, a biplane with upper and lower wings arched so that the tips nearly touched each other, got off the ice for more than 100 yards of uncontrolled flight before crash-landing. Team member Casey Baldwin flew it, and the Curtiss engine churned out ample power. Hundreds of people braved the cold to watch this "first *public* flight in the United States."

The AEA quickly built the White Wing, with the first wheels for takeoff and landing and the first ailerons to control bank. Casey Baldwin, then Tom Selfridge got better than 200 feet out of it. Then it was time for quiet Glenn Curtiss. With no instruction except advice from the others, he flew more than 1,000 feet. He was hooked.

Next project was the June Bug, with Curtiss in charge of design and construction. He wanted more speed — as always — so he reduced the wingspan of the earlier planes and increased the size of those ailerons. He flew it beautifully and then, on July 4, went public with it, going after the *Scientific American* trophy for a flight of one kilometer. People came to Hammondsport from miles away to watch Curtiss fly about a mile to win.

Bell's son-in-law, botanist David Fairchild, described vividly the way human flight seemed back in 1908.

Ever the speed merchant, Glenn set records with his "moto-cycles" like that pictured on this card to his wife.

"There was a sharp loud whirr and a cloud of dust and smoke as the blades of the propeller churned in the air.... The men holding the gigantic bird let go. It started down the track on its

Curtiss built his beautiful flying boat, America, *to cross the Atlantic. World War I intervened but in 1919, the NC-4, a larger version, made the epochal flight.*

rubbertired wheels...glided upward into the air and bored down upon us...like a gigantic ochre-colored condor carrying its prey. Soon the thin, strong features of the man, his bare outstretched arms and hands on the steering wheel, his legs on the bar in front, riveted our attention. Hemmed in by bars and wires, with a 40-horsepower engine exploding behind him leaving a trail of smoke and with a whirling propeller cutting the air 1,200 times a minute, he sailed with 40 feet of outstretched wings 20 feet above our heads."

In aviation circles, Curtiss was now famous. Even the reclusive Wrights took notice of the little June Bug — especially since they considered its control surfaces an infringement on their patent. If those ailerons of Glenn's could be considered a form of wing-warping, he'd be liable. Curtiss knew it was only a matter of time before legal artillery would be aimed at him.

After the AEA's final plane, the Silver Dart, flew successfully from the ice of the Bras d'Or Lakes — the first airplane flight in Canada — Curtiss eased out of Bell's brotherhood.

It had been a joyful interlude, working as one of the "boys" of the brilliant inventor and his wife. But a light went out of the Association when Tom Selfridge died. The young Army lieutenant had been assigned to ride with Orville in a Wright plane that would soon be accepted by the Army. A structural failure fouled a propeller and the plane crashed, badly injuring Orv and killing Tom — the first fatal accident in American aviation.

Curtiss sold his engine company to Octave Chanute's old assistant, Augustus Herring, who knew how to lure New York money. The new Herring-Curtiss Company offered Glenn a chance to get rich out of the air races and exhibition flights that were being scheduled in Europe and America. Flying was in a boom and Curtiss wanted to ride it, even though the Wrights were threatening to sue.

He called his first plane, built by Herring-Curtiss, the Gold Bug. It was small, built for speed. Its ailerons were set between the upper and lower wings. That way, the law might judge them clear of the patent coverage.

Then he went to France with a new, untested version of the Gold Bug, called the Racer, in time for the great air meet of 1909 at Reims.

The climax of its eight events was the race for the Gordon Bennett Trophy — "the best speed record by an airplane over a closed course." Curtiss aimed only for that prize. The betting was on Louis Bleriot, recent conqueror of the English Channel, but Curtiss proved to be a great curiosity to the French crowd. They'd never seen such an aviator. He actually worked on his plane beside his mechanics, toiling away in shirtsleeves, oil-smeared and sweaty!

On the great day, summer heat produced turbulence which battered the aircraft. But Curtiss, shaving the pylons like a motorcycle racer, beat Bleriot by six full seconds. Still shy, ever serious, Glenn became the hero of the day, constantly badgered by reporters. But at this time, too, the Wright's lawsuit was finally filed.

The legal war dragged on for years, enriching the lawyers. During injunctions and appeals, Curtiss could take to the air. But the years before World War I were difficult. Herring was discredited and their firm went bankrupt.

Curtiss started a new company in his hometown of Hammondsport, New York. He continued to produce such distinctive aircraft as the Headless Pusher, in which the rear-mounted engine "pushed" and the pilot sat out in front with nothing ahead of him, and the first successful flying boats. His planes and engines were everywhere. He set up flying schools. He continued to compete against a host of new European pilots as well as fellow Americans.

World War I loaded his firm with orders. His most memorable plane was the JN, the Jenny that trained thousands of pilots. In 1917, the huge Curtiss plant also started work on the NCs, great naval seaplanes designed to fly across the Atlantic. That notion dated back to 1912, when Curtiss' "hydroaeroplanes" proved a success. "I have taken a great interest in...a flight across the ocean," said Curtiss, "and I am willing to undertake the construction of a machine for the purpose."

The four NCs (called, naturally, Nancys) were four-engined flying boats with tail sections held high off the water by booms. With 126-foot wingspans they were the largest planes built in America up to that time.

Their chance came in 1919, thanks partly to the eager endorsement of the Assistant Secretary of the Navy, young Franklin D. Roosevelt. NC-2 got damaged by a gale before the start and was used only to provide spare parts for the other three. NC-4 had to land off Cape Cod for repairs but then caught up with the others. NC-1 and NC-3 were forced down on the way to the Azores.

Just a year before Glenn died, the business deal that had been a distant dream among aviation people took place. The mammoth Curtiss Aeroplane and Motor Corporation merged with the Wright Aeronautical Corporation, forming Curtiss-Wright, a powerful industrial giant headquartered in Dayton, Ohio — without patent infringements to worry about.

But apparently even the long hoped-for merger didn't thaw the ice between Glenn Curtiss and Orville Wright. When he read the new corporation's title, the latter complained because his name came second! ∎

Curtiss lands at Governor's Island, New York (above) to win $10,000 for the longest flight yet. He'd already garnered the splendid Scientific American *trophy (right) and the much-prized Gordon Bennett (far right) in Rheims, France. His Jenny graces a U.S. airmail stamp (near right) issued in 1918.*

But NC-4 went the distance, ending up finally in Plymouth, England.

Glenn Curtiss lived until 1930, and his name is forever associated with record-breaking aircraft. His series of Army and Navy racers set marks in the early '20s; their design inspired the Curtiss Hawk, for years a well-loved standard fighter for both the Army and the Navy.

BLANCHE STUART SCOTT

The aviation fad erupted in France in 1908 and soon swept to America. Everyone wanted to watch a plane fly; the more daring wanted to get a ride; the foolhardy wanted to learn how. The very first American woman to actually fly a plane by herself was Blanche Scott.

When Wilbur Wright was exhibiting his two-place model at Le Mans, in France, people of all stations in life — and of both sexes — besieged him.

"Princes & millionaires are as thick as fleas," he wrote to his brother Orville. In fact, Germany's Crown Prince Friedrich Wilhelm went up with Wilbur, and King Alfonso XIII of Spain would have gone if his wife had let him.

Not all wives were against flying. The spouse of the Wrights' agent in France, Hart O. Berg, got a ride with Wilbur and is remembered as the first woman to go up in a plane. Apparently, Mrs. Berg also gets credit for inspiring a new fashion. Before Wilbur took off with her, he saw to it that her voluminous skirt was wrapped with twine to keep it from blowing in the wind.

It's an indication of how intensely flight was admired that the hobbled skirt quickly became the rage. Soon, modish women of that Edwardian era were mincing around in skirts designed to look as though they were tied in preparation for a flight.

The Wrights also took up their sister Katharine. But it probably didn't occur to them to teach her to fly. Flying was dangerous and uncomfortable. Because the engine often sprayed gobs of hot oil, flying was also hard on the clothes. It was a man's job, the brothers believed. A woman's place was certainly not in the cockpit of an airplane.

Glenn Curtiss felt much the same way. He wasn't a bit happy when a perky, feisty redhead named Blanche Stuart Scott showed up at his Keuka Lake Field in Hammondsport, New York, in the summer of 1910. She wanted flying lessons.

Blanche was in her twenties, an attractive and adventurous young woman from a well-to-do family in nearby Rochester. She'd always had a startlingly masculine yen for bicycles, engines and autos. She'd practiced stunts on bikes all over Rochester and learned to drive the family Cadillac at age 13. Even "finishing school," as it was called back then, failed to cleanse the grease out of her bloodstream.

Never overly impressed by important strangers, Blanche Scott had accosted John Willys of the Willys Overland Company with the suggestion that she become the first woman to drive across the United States, coast to coast. She'd stop at company dealerships from New York to San Francisco, and the publicity would be great for car sales.

Willys went for it. On May 16, 1910, Blanche headed west in an Overland 28, following a winding course of more than 5,000 miles. That would be no cinch. Most roads were rutted wagon tracks, and in barely settled regions of the West they were apt to degenerate into buffalo wallows.

Soon after getting under way on her historic trek, Blanche and the woman journalist who accompanied her got snarled in a huge traffic jam in Dayton, Ohio, home of the Wright brothers, and hence a shrine city of aviation.

Brochure of Blanche Scott's 5,000-mile automobile trek across the United States indicates the fame she gained in 1910. Then the flying bug infected her.

Issued:
December 30, 1980
Hammondsport, NY

The tieup was caused by an air show at the Wright flying school, and Blanche had time to look at the planes banking overhead. Her newspaper friend reported that she refused to get overly impressed. Even meeting the famous brothers failed to give her the flying bug. Her adventure was on the open road, not above it.

Upon her triumphant arrival in California more than three months later, Blanche was lionized. Among many gifts and honors showered upon her was the offer of a ride in a Farman biplane with Charles F. Willard, the first student pilot Glenn Curtiss had taught and now a talented exhibition flyer. Blanche agreed to be his passenger on a flight from San Diego to Tijuana, Mexico, and back. She had

made a name for herself, as well as for Willys Overland, and realized that she now was sought after by admirers who saw possibilities for publicity.

Scott's first flight, however, failed to come off because a gale destroyed the plane. But a newsman had already broken the story back East, and when it was splashed in the papers, Blanche decided to live with it.

The result was that after she had returned to New York, Willard's boss, Jerome Fanciulli, who was head of Glenn Curtiss' exhibition flying team, asked Miss Scott how she felt about continuing to fly. She'd proved she could do it, so how about becoming a pilot, even joining up with the Curtiss air show? She was caught then. She couldn't say no.

Young Blanche pays close attention to her instructor, Glenn Curtiss (back to camera), as he tells her to practice taxiing at Hammondsport, NY. She taxied fast enough to leave the ground — the first woman to solo.

Armed with Fanciulli's recommendation, Blanche Scott appeared at Keuka Lake Field. Glenn Curtiss looked her over dubiously — all 5' 1" of her — and agreed to take her on as his own student. She was the only woman he ever taught to fly.

In those days, flight training was simple: start by taxiing, first very carefully, then at a good speed —"grass-cutting," it was called. The mechanics blocked the throttle so the student couldn't get power enough to take off.

But on September 2, 1910, that throttle block apparently came loose — either all by itself or with a little help from the pilot, the impatient Miss Scott. Before anyone knew it, there was Blanche, 40 feet in the air and doing just fine. After landing, she explained that a gust of wind had lifted her off.

Scott's little flight made her the first woman to solo in the United States. But since the Aeronautical Society considered it accidental, the honor of being "First American Aviatrix" went to Bessica Raiche.

Originally from Beloit, Wisconsin, Bessica was the wife of a French aviator.

She was a brilliant, restless woman, a musician, artist and scholar who consistently joined in men's sporting activities and often outdid them. She was a fine shot, for example. Two weeks after Blanche Scott's solo flight, Bessica also soloed in a Wright-type plane that she and her husband had built largely in their living room.

Glenn Curtiss couldn't care less which woman was first. As far as he was concerned, neither should have been in a cockpit. But he knew Blanche Scott was a natural. A month after her solo, Curtiss let his headstrong pupil join one of his teams of stunt flyers.

Off went Blanche to Chicago to take part in the 1910 air meet there, in October. No hobbled skirt for her. She wore bloomers — the mid-19th-century invention of Mrs. Amelia Jenks Bloomer of New York. These big, baggy pants allowed a woman to be physically active and remain "decent." Though not exactly fetching in appearance, bloomers served perfectly to foil the blast of the slipstream.

Soon after Scott's debut, she broke away from the troupe to marry. Her husband had helped with her auto trip, acting as advance man and making life as easy for her as possible.

It's unlikely that "The Tomboy of the Air" ever flew in a cyclone, but a flying circus ran on "hype" (above). Sweatered against the slipstream's blast, the redoubtable Miss Scott, barely more than five feet tall, takes her seat in a Curtiss Pusher (opposite).

She was his devoted bride for a while, but flying had gotten to her. In July 1911, she joined Curtiss' old friend Thomas Scott Baldwin in his show at Mineola, New York. This was the "Captain" Baldwin whose dirigible was the first to fly successfully in the United States. It was a primitive affair, its nose pointing up or down as the pilot moved back and forth along its narrow catwalk.

One day Blanche, who had the temper to go with her red hair, got into a steaming argument with Captain Baldwin over some small matter. Too angry to speak, she stormed out onto the flying field, got into her plane, and swept off on a straight course.

Nervously, Baldwin and the mechanics waited for her to return. Flying in 1910 consisted of making circuits around a field, not whizzing off over the horizon. Baldwin sent word around that part of Long Island to watch out for an airplane wreck.

Finally Miss Scott reappeared, anger gone, innocently unaware of the fuss she'd caused. She'd flown over Central Islip and back, and a news reporter splashed the story that Blanche Scott held the distance record — about 60 miles — for women.

Touring all over the United States with Baldwin, Blanche developed her daredevil flying routines. "The Tomboy of The Air," shrilled a handbill, luring her fans to watch her among "14 Nerve-Tingling, Spine-Chilling, Thrill-Producing Events Every Day." Booted, gaitered and bloomer-clad, little Blanche would swing past each eager crowd, inverted, 20 feet off the ground.

She'd run through her repertoire, never quailing at occasionally darting under a handy bridge. She is sometimes pictured in a Curtiss Pusher with forward elevator — the Gold Bug model. But at the time of her return to exhibition flight, the more spectacular Headless Pusher was being developed at Curtiss, and Scott may well have flown it.

Blanche Scott's most famous and "Nerve-Tingling" maneuver was her "Death Dive." She'd climb to 4,000 feet, then nose over and come straight down. At the last second she'd ease out of this chilling plunge. Sometimes she only had a couple of hundred feet to spare.

Blanche got through all such routines safely, earning as much as $5,000 per week from salary and her percentage of the gate. But in 1913, on the last day of May, she was in Madison, Wisconsin, doing some low-altitude stunts

in a Red Devil, a Curtiss-like plane that Baldwin had recently designed. She heard a crack and found that a wing cable had snapped.

Suddenly out of control, the plane spiraled down and plowed into a swamp. It was a good place to hit because Blanche got away with only an injury to her shoulder that grounded her for some months.

When she returned to flying almost a year later, she continued putting on her shows. But she also accepted jobs testing aircraft for both Curtiss and Glenn Martin. She could later lay claim to being the first woman test pilot.

Then abruptly, in 1916, Blanche Scott quit. She was still a very hot pilot even though she'd broken a total of 41 bones in various crackups. But, as she said, aviation itself seemed to be changing, and her part in it had taken on a grim overtone.

"In aviation there seems to be no place for the woman engineer, mechanic, or flyer," she said regretfully. "Too often people paid money to see me risk my neck, more as a freak — a woman freak pilot — than as a skilled flyer. No more!"

Blanche was married three times. The first two didn't stick, though the breakups were amicable. She and her third husband ran a movie production studio on Long Island for a number of years, an outlet for her bent toward show business. After his death she worked in Hollywood as a screenwriter for 14 years. Finally she returned to her native Rochester, originating her own radio program. She was a popular fixture for many years. She also handled public relations for the U.S. Air Force Museum in Dayton, Ohio, making several television appearances to raise money. Many honors came to her before her death in 1970.

One was another first, scored when she was taken up in an F-80, the Lockheed Shooting Star. She was the first woman to ride as passenger in a jet fighter. She did it on the anniversary of her first, controversial solo flight. ∎

Blanche survived early barnstorming to end up as a Hollywood screenwriter.

HARRIET QUIMBY

Blanche Scott wasn't alone in noting a new and unhealthy attitude, beginning around 1910, in America's nonflying public. Many pilots remembered that when they'd started, people crowded to the fair grounds and race tracks because flight was a miracle. Wilbur Wright told of seeing a witness of one of brother Orville's aerial displays in 1909. The man walked away afterward in a daze, murmuring "My God! My God!"

But as the Glenn Curtiss and Wright brothers teams competed in daring stunts, the dark side of human nature appeared. When the Wright pilot, Ralph Johnstone, failed to pull out of a dive at an air meet in Denver (where the air is thin), the crowd swarmed upon the wreck and tore bits of clothing from his battered body. The feeling grew among flyers that what all those excited fans really wanted was the spectacle of sudden death.

Young Hap Arnold, later to become Commanding General of the U.S. Army Air Forces in World War II, watched America's first international air meet at Belmont, New York, in 1910. He noted that people "gaped at the wonders, the exhibits of planes from home and abroad, secure in the knowledge that nowhere on earth, between now and suppertime, was there such a good chance of seeing somebody break his neck."

Or *her* neck. Women were entering the field of aviation, and the first one to get a pilot's license was lissome, green-eyed Harriet Quimby. She remains in the record books as the first woman to fly the English Channel.

Talented, beautiful Harriet Quimby poses fetchingly in her flying costume — plum-colored, wool-lined satin with a hood. She designed it herself, and because of posters like this, it became a trademark. So did the Bleriot-type monoplane in the background. She flew these for Moisant International Aviators before her Channel flight.

Harriet had no trouble talking someone into giving her flight instruction. She was an exciting, glamorous woman, a drama critic for *Leslie's Weekly*, and she'd met an exciting, glamorous pilot named John Moisant. He was brave and rich. His family was into sugar in Central America and banking in New York.

Johnny brought a Bleriot monoplane to the 1910 Belmont Park Aviation Meet to help defend the Gordon Bennett Trophy which Glenn Curtiss had previously won. After the final day of the Belmont meet, Moisant showed up at a dinner party and met Harriet Quimby, looking fetching.

"Teach me to fly," begged Harriet.

"Anytime," answered Johnny.

And then, tragically, on the last day of 1910, Moisant was killed in a crash.

Harriet hadn't really known him very well but she'd made friends with his sister, Matilde, and she'd never forgotten about learning to fly. So when the Moisant Aviation School opened at Hempstead, Long Island, the following April, both Harriet and Matilde were among its first students.

When asked about her background, Harriet Quimby dropped discreet hints about a girlhood as the daughter of a wealthy family in California, about private schooling in Europe. But that was part of a game her determinedly ambitious mother had put her up to. In reality, her father was a Michigan farmer who had served as a cook in the Union army during the Civil War. Failing to make much of a go of the land, William Quimby moved his family to California, where he was sure he'd get rich. He ended up selling bottles of medicine. Harriet and her sister actually received their formal education in public schools.

Harriet Quimby was bright as well as beautiful. Her first job was in San Francisco, writing for the *Dramatic Review*, with sometimes a feature for the *Chronicle*. In 1903, year of the Wright brothers' success, she got her New York job with *Leslie's Weekly*.

Knowing that flying would give her an unfailingly popular subject for features, Harriet doggedly pursued her pilot's license.

She spent four months getting 33 lessons in a monoplane designed after the famous Bleriot that had flown the English Channel. She then tackled the final requirement, a spot landing. She had to touch down within 100 feet of where she'd left the ground on takeoff, a task deceivingly difficult in the unwieldy aircraft of the day.

She missed on the first day. But on August 1, 1911, she touched less than eight feet from the spot and became the first American woman to carry a pilot's certificate — No. 37. Less than two weeks later, her best friend, Matilde Moisant, became the second licensed woman flyer in the U.S.

Harriet was quickly snapped up by Moisant International Aviators, an exhibition group that the family sponsored. She entered a New York meet, won a race, toured down to Mexico, and became the first woman to fly over Mexico City.

All this gave her material for her magazine. Quimby articles included "How I Won My Aviator's License" and "The Dangers of Flying." She sounded a call for more women in this new field: "I see no reason why they cannot realize handsome incomes by carrying passengers between adjacent towns, why they cannot derive incomes from parcel delivery, from taking photographs from above, or from conducting schools for flying."

Issued:
April 27, 1991
Plymouth, MI

She became known for her flying suit. She had designed it herself — plum-colored satin backed by wool, with a monk's cowl that kept her hair in place and her ears warm. Her almond-shaped goggles were years ahead of their time.

Leslie's Weekly put up money for her to fly the English Channel. The *London Daily Mirror* helped out, and away Harriet went. An Englishwoman stole a little of Harriet's thunder by being "the first woman to fly across the Channel" — but only as a passenger. Being "first woman pilot" to make the crossing was something else.

The man who'd flown that passenger across didn't think Harriet could do it. Entranced by her as were most men, he offered a wealth of advice, ending with the suggestion that he don her plum-colored flying suit and go in her place.

Harriet laughed him off, but when she took off on a dank April day in 1912, she was grateful for the last thing he gave her — a hot-water bottle.

In the air or on the ground, Harriet won male hearts. She was ever a hard-nosed journalist, quick to fashion feature articles from her adventures. Ironically, her own tragic death made the most gripping tale of all.

This was a hot story, and Quimby told it well for *Fly* magazine: "The noise of the motor drowned the shouts and cheers of friends below. In a moment I was in the air, climbing steadily in a long circle.... From this high point of vantage my eyes lit at once on Dover Castle. It was half hidden in a fog bank. I felt that trouble was coming, but I made directly for the flagstaff of the castle, as I had promised the waiting *Mirror* photographers and the moving-picture men I should do...."

She swept beyond the white cliffs, passed the *Mirror*'s chartered tug, then "the quickening fog obscured my view." Fortunately she at least had a compass and had learned how to use it. She held course with it while searching through the haze for land.

"My hands were covered with long, Scotch woolen gloves, which gave me good protection from the cold and fog, but the machine was wet and my face was so covered with dampness that I had to push my goggles up on my forehead," she noted.

Realizing that land must be in sight, she dropped from 2,000 feet to about 1,000 and broke into sunlight over the shoreline of France.

Harriet missed her target of Calais but landed safely on the beach and was swamped by a joyous crowd. It should have been a great news piece for the *Daily Mirror*. The trouble was, just as she made her flight, word of the *Titanic* ship-sinking disaster hit the wires and stole the headlines.

Still, Quimby — aviation's "Dresden Doll" — was feted by flyers and was asked to take part in exhibitions and meets. In June 1912, she arrived at Squantum Airfield, south of Boston, for the Harvard-Boston Aviation Meet where, the year before, the heralded Glenn Curtiss had vied with Britain's Claude Grahame-White and for once had to make do with second place.

In 1912, the meet drew a mixed bag of hot pilots — Charlie Hamilton, a hard-drinking daredevil; the matchless stuntman Lincoln Beachey, who once flew through a huge building (deliberately) in San Francisco; Glenn Martin; Blanche Scott, and of course Harriet Quimby, in a new, all-white, two-seater Bleriot that a lot of European pilots thought was unstable. She flew passengers around and talked of going after Grahame-White's speed mark.

Late on the second day, she took up William Willard, manager of the meet and father of Charles Willard, the Curtiss pilot with whom Blanche Scott had supposedly first flown. They went out over Boston Harbor to Boston Light and then returned. The white monoplane circled, gleaming against the summer sky as it started to let down. Then, abruptly, it nosed over and dove.

A joyous French crowd bears Harriet Quimby triumphantly to shore on April 16, 1912, after her flight from England ended on a Normandy beach near their village of Hardelot, 25 miles from Calais. News of the Titanic *disaster robbed her of headlines she deserved for being the first woman to cross the English Channel.*

Another woman, however, witnessed the tragedy and went on to become one of America's most famous pilots of all time. She was Ruth Law, destined to set a nonstop long-distance record for men as well as women and gain lasting fame. Ruth had just joined a flying school in Boston, on the day of Harriet Quimby's death, and was on her first flight when she saw Harriet fall.

Despite that chilling sight, Ruth kept at it, learning, perfecting, "pushing at the envelope." That's what aviation pioneers do, men and women alike. ■

"The Dresden China Aviatrix" poses in a Bleriot XI. This was the type in which she made her historic flight across the English Channel, and it was in a similar plane that Quimby met her death. Note the lack of a seat belt.

To the horror of the huge crowd, William was flung upward from the rear seat. His body described an arc and fell 1,000 feet into the shallow water of a tidal mud flat. The plane seemed to come under control for a moment. Then it turned over and Quimby, too, fell from it, the afternoon sun etching her tumbling body in its flying suit as she hurtled to her death. Pilotless, the Bleriot straightened out and landed with little damage.

Blanche Scott was flying at the time, trying for a duration award. She saw the accident and, said a newspaper, "turned the nose of her machine downward, came to a landing like a flash, and swooned before anyone could reach her side."

There was enormous speculation about the cause of Harriet's death. Some thought that Willard had momentarily forgotten the injunction to sit still and had leaned forward, half-rising from his seat to speak to Harriet. He was a big man, and the shift of his weight might have caused the nose of the plane to drop before Quimby could catch it. Others thought something had become entangled in the control wires or that Harriet, like Blanche, had swooned. Swooning was always considered a possibility for the woman of 1912.

Aviator Glenn Martin later remarked that some sort of seat belt might have saved two lives.

Harriet's great friend, dimpled Matilde Moisant, had set altitude records and proved herself a daredevil. But a dangerous crash which she barely survived in April 1912, combined with Harriet's death, was enough to persuade Matilde to give it up.

Englishmen hold back the Bleriot as Harriet runs up the engine. Lacking brakes, the plane strains to start across the Channel. A British aviator kneels over the cockpit to give Quimby a few final words — including an offer to swap clothes and take her place.

LAWRENCE & ELMER SPERRY

Clouds have socked in over the airport, but the great jets keep right on flying. One by one, the "heavies" rumble into the whiteness and disappear. Their passengers look out into a wall of fog. Their pilots monitor the effortless, absolutely accurate climbs and turns of the monstrous airplanes even though the fog is just as thick from where they sit.

The secret to this miracle of blind flight is a sophisticated system of electronics and instrumentation that in essence takes control of the airplane.

And these futuristic developments trace their ancestry to the principle of the gyroscope — that vertical spinning wheel which tries to hold its direction no matter how its base is twisted and turned about. In aviation's early days, a father and one — sometimes two — of his sons invented, developed and experimented with instruments and control devices based on that gyroscope.

Genius seldom passes directly from father to son. When it does, fireworks are likely. That was the way of the

Ever fascinated by gyroscopes, inventor Elmer Sperry (above) developed flight instruments and stabilizers from them. His madcap son Lawrence flew as a boy before learning properly (opposite).

Sperry family. Elmer Ambrose Sperry — the name goes back to the settlement of New England in the 1600s — studied engineering and then felt the excitement that seemed to grip the world at the dawn of the 20th century.

This was a time when human capabilities surged, the ceilings of ambition rose. Anything was possible — the abstractions of Picasso, the experimental writings of Gertrude Stein, instant communication by telephone, quick transportation by automobile and, at long last, even flight.

Little wonder that in such a heady environment, Elmer Sperry broke away from a secure engineering job and struck out on his own.

Sperry, a conservative, properly dressed businessman with a perpetually quizzical cast to his eyebrows, flaunted convention and set himself up as an inventor. He worked with electricity and industrial uses for chemistry, then suddenly saw great possibilities for that mysterious gyroscopic force that keeps wanting to maintain its own stability. So among his more than 400 patents are the gyroscopic compass and the gyroscopic stabilizer for the great ocean liners of the day.

Elmer had accomplished a good deal of his inventing by 1903 and paid scant attention to the Wrights' first flight. But the news from Kitty Hawk electrified his three sons, especially the middle one, Lawrence, aged 11. He was a mechanical whiz kid and quickly followed the Wrights' example by opening a bike repair shop in the basement of the Sperry's home. In 1910, abetted by his younger brother, Elmer Jr., he began building a glider.

This activity wasn't so strange in those days. Hundreds of boys read instructions in such magazines as *Popular Mechanics* and got the aviation bug. The Sperry parents shrugged off their son's enthusiasm as normal.

But they didn't know Lawrence as well as they thought. During summer vacation, when mother and daughter were at a resort and father was away on business, Lawrence and young Elmer finished the glider's wings and set about moving them to the backyard for assembly. But — oops — the wings were too big. They tried the largest window — the bay window of the master bedroom. No go.

Obviously, there was only one thing to do: get some tools and demolish that window. The elder Sperrys returned to a partially destroyed home. The two boys were sorry... but, hey! Look at that beautiful glider in the backyard!

Young Lawrence soon flew the glider. It worked fine. Then he lined up an engine, an Anzani five-cylinder, 60-horsepower radial, by floating a loan.

When school opened that fall of 1910, he and young Elmer played hooky from classes for the first week in order to mount the engine at a neighboring race track. Lawrence then started it up, got his plane into the air, made some turns, and landed it without cracking it up. And even though the authorities descended on him — thin-lipped school principal, distraught mother, perturbed father — Lawrence knew that somehow, someday he would be a flyer.

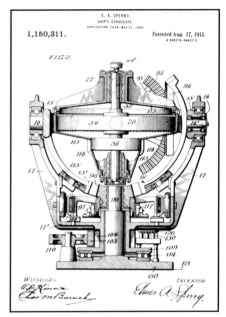

Elmer Sperry's patent drawing of a ship's gyroscope of 1908 shows its essential arrangement. Centrifugal force of the rapidly spinning wheel resists changes of course and buffeting by waves. In aircraft, this stabilizing effect allowed the first "hands-off" flying.

Issued:
February 13, 1985
Garden City, NY

Handy little Sperry Messenger, designed by Fred Verville to meet Billy Mitchell's needs, could seemingly land anywhere safely, including — with skis — snow-covered fields.

Elmer Sperry senior tried to aim Lawrence at Cornell. But the boy coerced his father into allowing him to join Glenn Curtiss — first as a student pilot, then as his father's representative in experiments on gyroscopic controls and instruments for aircraft.

A spoiled rich man's son he may have been, but everyone liked Lawrence Sperry — known later as "Gyro" Sperry. Glenn Curtiss noted that Lawrence never needed dual instruction: "He was *born* to fly." At age 20 he became the country's youngest licensed flyer, earning certificate No. 11 as a hydroplane pilot and soon qualifying on all types. He was a handsome youth, 6' 2", with a ready smile. Women adored him.

Supervised by the Navy, Lawrence began perfecting his innovative father's aerial gyroscopic stabilizer. In place of an engineering background, the indefatigable son had the pragmatic instinct to try every device and development himself, in the air.

Two gyroscopes were supposed to react to the pitching up or down of the plane and its roll from side to side. Lawrence put them at the plane's center of gravity and linked them with servomotors that would move the controls. Then he watched their reactions, again and again, while a Navy pilot sat at the controls. The trouble was, that pilot didn't trust the gyros and would take over the controls before they had a chance to do their stuff.

A determined Lawrence Sperry knew the logical solution to that problem. One Sunday morning, too early for the Curtiss people to be up, he took the hydroplane up alone. Circling, he lay on the floorboards beside his gyroscopes, where he could reach the rudder pedals. Then he threw the plane off course with a shove and watched the gyros bring it back. Occasionally he found time to stick his head out and see that he wasn't headed straight for the moon, the planet earth, or another early bird!

Glenn Curtiss was roused by a guard, who said, "Boss, there's a plane up there without a pilot." Curtiss got up and watched Lawrence at work, and after the young man landed, Curtiss told him they were going to France to enter an aircraft safety competition.

At Bezons, near Paris, Lawrence hired a French mechanic, a hardy little man named Emile who, as Lawrence wrote to his father, "doesn't need to be told what to do." The two got the Curtiss flying boat with its gyrostabilizer ready for testing and found themselves the last of 57 entries. The elder Sperry showed up to watch and invited naval attachés of all leading nations.

When their great moment came, young Sperry and Emile took off from the Seine and headed for the crowd. As they approached, flying low, Lawrence stood up in the cockpit, holding both hands over his head. On the second pass over the judges, Emile walked out on one wing while Lawrence again held his hands high. The plane dipped momentarily, then righted itself. Third time around, Emile moved back on the fuselage to throw it off balance. Again the plane leveled out with no help from the pilot.

In an early Curtiss flying boat cockpit, gyrostabilizer, low in foreground, was mounted to control the plane. Demonstrating his dad's device in France, Lawrence lifted his hands off the wheel while his mechanic wing-walked. Gyros quickly leveled the plane.

Landing, the pair were lionized. They had won a prize amounting to $10,000 and set what a French paper rightly called a "historic date in aerial navigation." Here was the birth of today's sophisticated automatic pilot that reduces many tasks on the flight deck of a giant airliner to mere monitoring. That particular historic date was June 18, 1914. Other events of that summer of 1914 erased it from memory, for two months later, the German army was storming through Belgium in an opening phase of the Great War.

The Sperry family prospered greatly from the gyrostabilizer and from the various contracts that flooded Elmer's business after war broke out. The boys worked faithfully for their dad, though Lawrence tried to join the Lafayette Escadrille. The Escadrille wouldn't take him because it wanted only college graduates. Bored, he scared New Yorkers by buzzing the East River bridges, devised retractible wheels for his flying boat, raised hackles by buzzing the

Statue of Liberty, and then was sent to England on stabilizer business.

He came home to find himself named to the Sperry staff as manager of the stabilizer department. But boredom with office work persisted. Also the inventive streak. Often he left his plush New York office to fly, and his many jaunts produced ideas — 26 patents were awarded him between 1915 and 1923. Among other things, pilots have him to thank for the turn-and-bank indicator — the essential "ball and needle" that has long been at the heart of instrument flying.

Finally, Lawrence set up his own Lawrence Sperry Aircraft Company, separate from his father's Sperry Gyroscope Company yet maintaining a close association. Lawrence acted as consultant and garnered royalties for the inventions that were his alone, such as the aerial torpedo, the turn indicator and the inclinometer.

His company built experimental planes — a sleek racer, a 1919 amphibian triplane with retractable wheels —

but young Sperry's most memorable aircraft was the Messenger, a small, single-seat biplane.

It was designed originally for Army training and liaison, but Lawrence used it to perpetuate the American dream of a "flying flivver." In the early '20s, many wondered if aviation couldn't become an everyday means of transportation, and the little Messenger was a tangible example. Lawrence kept his in his Long Island garage, flew it every day to his office, landed easily on unfrequented highways, visited the golf club in it and, on a trip to Washington, landed in front of the Capitol and ran it up the steps.

The Royal Air Force wanted to look the Messenger over, so Lawrence Sperry shipped it to Britain in 1923. Then Dutch and French airmen got interested, so Sperry planned an easy Channel flight to Amsterdam.

He took off from Croydon on a cold December day, flew down over Kent and Sussex, and disappeared.

In mid-January 1924, a body washed up on the Channel coast. Elmer Jr. identified it as his brother's. Probably Lawrence tried to swim ashore, only to have the bitter cold of the English Channel defeat him as it did so many wartime airmen who had to bail out into it 20 years later.

Elmer Sperry continued to make instruments that would take much of the danger out of flying. Elmer Jr. now became his good right arm. It was young Elmer who worked closely with Jimmy Doolittle to develop the instruments for totally blind flight. They achieved success in 1929 when Doolittle took off from Mitchell Field on Long Island in a dense fog, flew blind for 10 minutes, and landed perfectly. Just like those great jets today. ∎

Lawrence Sperry used his own Sperry Messenger like a motor scooter, landing it on golf courses and roads. In 1922, irked by the Navy's laxness in settling a bill from his company, he flew to Washington, buzzed the Capitol, touched down on a plaza, and finished his landing run by bumping up the Capitol steps. His bill was paid.

ALFRED V. VERVILLE

T he appealing little biplane which Lawrence Sperry built and flew everywhere, and in which he lost his life, owed most of its design to Alfred Victor Verville. It's sometimes called the Verville-Sperry Messenger, but usual practice has been to use only the builder's name — not the designer's. So Verville is hardly a household name. Actually, it's French-Canadian. Fred's parents crossed over the border to Michigan before he was born in 1890.

He learned electrical engineering through a correspondence course, a humble start to a career as one of American aviation's most famous "back-room boys." Those were the engineer-designers who, far from the limelight, drew their dream planes on paper, supervised their construction, then let the pilots wring them out and garner the applause.

Fred Verville's dreams were a decade ahead of their time, but he developed a succession of aircraft, usually on short notice and a tight budget, that were marvels. Without him, this country's aviation history wouldn't be the same.

He got his first job at the Ford Motor Company at age 21. After stints at Hudson Motors and then an Edison electric plant, he was drawn — as were so many other bright, modern-minded youngsters — to Hammondsport, New York, where Glenn Curtiss was becoming the guru of early flight.

In aviator's garb, Alfred Victor Verville poses beside an early bird. Generally, Fred wore a suit, for his career was at the drawing board, not the controls.

Curtiss always needed good engineers and had a ready task for this short, affable, quietly competent newcomer with electrical know-how: rig a searchlight on the experimental flying boat *America*, so a mechanic could work on the engines at night while crossing the Atlantic. Verville succeeded but World War I kept Curtiss' *America* from making that historic flight.

War orders then poured into Hammondsport. Caught up in the excitement, young Verville decided he ought to learn to fly. Glenn Curtiss dissuaded him. "There are a hundred pilots for every good engineer," said Curtiss, and Fred took the advice. He also felt confident enough in his career to move on.

He tried working for Thomas Morse, who later would produce one of the very few American fighters built for World War I (it never saw combat). Fred got better pay but soon decided

The pressing need for armament brought big players into the game. General Aeroplane found itself playing hardball with General Motors.

Since Verville couldn't lick 'em, he joined 'em. In 1917 he closed his shop and went to work for the Fisher Body Division of GM. His first task was to adapt the De Havilland DH-4, Britain's all-around attack plane, for American flyers to feel at home with once they started flying in France.

At war's end, the Army Air Service invited Verville to join an inspection tour of France to see the latest designs in fighter aircraft. He returned to the Army's flight research center at McCook Field. This Dayton, Ohio, airdrome was near Huffman Prairie, where the Wrights had done five years of testing and perfecting after their first flight in 1903. It became as famous in the 1920s as did Edwards Air Force Base in California for its involvement in

Issued:
February 13, 1985
Garden City, NY

It, too, was husky and powerful, with a 300-H.P. Hispano engine. Unfortunately, it also was heavy and not very nimble. Visibility was poor, too. But it was *fast!*

And the Army was interested in the speed being developed at McCook. Now that those thrilling, hyped-up air battles between flamboyant aces were over, air races appeared about the only way to keep aviation in the public eye. So Fred Verville was put to work turning his VCP-1 into the VCP-R (for racer). He packed a 600-H.P. Packard engine into it and entered it in the 1920 Gordon Bennett races. It overheated and dropped out. But in that year's race for the Pulitzer trophy, the VCP-R posted an average speed of 156.5 miles per hour and came away the winner. Verville's reputation was made.

Fred's next notable plane was the Messenger that Lawrence Sperry so loved — and which he finally ditched in the fatally cold English Channel. It had been the idea of General Billy Mitchell, home from the war and trumpeting the need for a separate American air force. Mitchell wanted a small, handy single-seater that could get in and out of cramped patches of rough ground. Such a plane would provide quick liaison and immediate artillery spotting when it was suddenly needed.

he'd be happier on his own. Early in 1915, he took the big step. His General Aeroplane Co. opened in Detroit and a year later produced a beautiful flying boat. Sensing the imminence of war, he also put together an experimental pusher plane that mounted a machine gun — an American adaptation of the British "gun bus." Unfortunately, it skidded out of control on frozen Lake St. Clair and cracked up.

With only one plane to show for a year's operation, General Aeroplane now faced the realities of the business world as American involvement in the Great War became probable.

"Give me tomorrow's plane today," said Billy Mitchell to Fred in 1924. Result: the R-3, with cantilevered wing and retractable wheels.

space shuttle efforts two generations later. Verville was caught up with McCook's pioneering experiments and burgeoning ideas.

He enthused about the latest SPADs he'd seen in France. These husky, effective fighters now had engines that topped 200 horsepower. The Army told him to design something as good for the United States. The result was an experimental fighter called the VCP-1.

So Mitchell's friend Lawrence Sperry built it — working from Fred Verville's design.

Impressed with Verville, Mitchell took him aside one day in 1921. "I want tomorrow's plane today," he said. "And I don't want any squirrel cage. Draw something up by morning."

Fred went to work and stayed at it all night before presenting Mitchell with a design that brought a whistle to the general's lips. Looking at a streamlined, low-wing monoplane with retracting wheels, Mitchell told Fred to build three of these futuristic planes in time for next year's Pulitzer trophy race.

Verville completed his design for this R-3 Racer, and again Sperry got the contract to build the planes. The wing had to be hefty enough to hold the retracted gear and the internal bracing — no "squirrel cage" of exterior wires allowed. That meant a thickness of about 18 inches at the wing root, and the center section would have to be wood, while the rest of the wingspan was fabric-covered.

Built this way, the wing showed a tendency to flutter. Verville then sacrificed lightness by covering the whole wing with thin plywood.

The nose of the aircraft was designed to take a new Curtiss engine. The Curtiss people, with their own racers slated to compete for the Pulitzer, wouldn't release the engine. Thus Verville had to make do with a Wright engine that had a reputation for vibrating.

Vibrate it did. Despite their ultra-modern look, the Verville-Sperry R-3s suffered enormous problems. Vibration knocked out most of the instruments and sent a piece of cowl flying. In a speed trial, the torque was so bad that the pilot, Fonda Johnson, had to use both feet on the right rudder. Trying a steep turn, Johnson rolled one-and-a-quarter times!

The three Verville planes still entered the race, but Johnson reported that he smelled his engine "cooking" even before the start. Then it got so hot that it preignited, and by the time he

crossed the finish line, sparks were showering from his exhaust. He averaged 178 mph for seventh place.

Gene Barksdale, piloting the second R-3, had much the same trouble but made 181 mph for fifth place. St. Clair Street, in the third Verville racer, broke an oil line and had to force-land.

All honors went to the Curtiss biplanes in 1922. But Verville tried again in '23, this time with the Curtiss engine in one plane. Vibration was no longer a problem, but at high speed the wing tended to warp, throwing the R-3 almost out of control. Fred beefed up the wing with a bit more wood and put a slightly different airfoil in each wing to straighten them out at high speed. He had time for only by guess and by golly, but it paid off. On a speed test, the R-3 hit 233 mph — close to a world record.

But again the low-wing monoplane couldn't match Curtiss' biplanes. Fred had to wait until 1924 before finally winning the Pulitzer with 215 mph — a disappointing showing, he felt.

He had proved, however, that his overnight design, slapped together in mere weeks and never completely tested, was the look of the future. If it hadn't been drawn up during the peaceful, prosperous '20s, when defense spending was minimal, U.S. Army fighter pilots might have been flying something like a Hawker Hurricane a full decade before that design was achieved in Britain.

Shouldered out of the way of big business, pinched by government parsimony, Fred Verville nevertheless gained distinction as a craftsman who built high-quality aircraft and could meet impossible challenges with breakthrough designs. In 1925, after a lively stint heading up McCook Field's "Pursuit and Racing Planes Projects," he resigned to enter private business again.

At the time, military research and experimentation was so underfunded as to be almost extinct. But sport and business flying seemed likely to boom. Fred formed a new company and produced a three-place biplane, the Airster — nice and conventional, just what people thought of when they heard the word "airplane."

Setting up the General Aeroplane Company in 1915, Verville built this beauty — a mahogany-hulled flying boat. It turned out to be his only product.

Verville's R-1 grew out of a SPAD-like fighter he designed for the Army in 1918. It was turned down, but with a 600-H.P. Packard motor, it became the speedster (above) that won the 1920 Pulitzer Race. Fred's most successful venture was the dainty little biplane (far right), called the AT Sportsman. Verville earlier adapted the De Havilland DH-4 (which appeared on a U.S. airmail stamp issued in 1923, shown at near right) for American flyers' use.

It was a good design but Fred seems to have been a little bored by it. He traveled in Europe again, came back with new ideas, and in 1927 produced the Verville Air Coach, a four-place cabin monoplane.

This was an expensive, quality aircraft, an early executive plane. Trouble was, the plane appeared in the year of the stock market crash.

Verville followed the Air Coach with the AT Sportsman, another popular standard biplane, and managed to sell 18 of them. The Sportsman had a 165-H.P. Continental engine, and with its two open cockpits resembled closely the Stearman biplanes in which World War II air cadets learned to fly.

It almost *was* that biplane trainer. With it, Verville won an Army competition for a primary trainer.

But the Army only bought four of the planes, designated YPT-10s. After all, the year was 1931 — the nadir of the Depression — and even the military was broke.

So ended Verville's last big chance. Even though a huge Army order was in the works, his backers pulled out and the designer suddenly had no company. The order for primary trainers went to Stearman.

Alfred Verville, recognized as one of the world's most brilliant aircraft designers, had to venture into the business of trailer homes after that. But as soon as he could swing it, even in that terrible economic climate, he returned to aviation. A valuable consultant, he worked for the State of Michigan as

well as the federal government, traveled to Europe and advised on museum collections, including the Smithsonian's National Air and Space Museum.

A few years before his death in 1970, Fred Verville saw his R-3 racer named as one of the most significant aircraft in the world. It deserved the honor, just as its designer deserves to have his own significance remembered. ■

IGOR SIKORSKY

Everyone interested in flying comes across, at some time, an old photograph of a monstrous airplane lumbering low over a bleak, wintry field with two men actually standing on its fuselage. That huge aircraft was the Russian Il'ya Muromets, on one of its momentous flights.

In those days, shortly before the first World War erupted in 1914, aviators considered four-engine planes foolhardy. Surely any loss of power by one of the engines would contort the aircraft and throw it into a fatal spin. But according to that old photo, some people had enough confidence in this particular aircraft to stand on its

Swinging confidently in midair, inventor Igor Sikorsky checks out a rescue hoist on one of his helicopters. He considered life-saving one of their major roles.

plywood "observation deck," their military greatcoats flapping in the slipstream. The designer of this giant, so radical for its day, was Igor Sikorsky, the 25-year-old whiz kid of Russian aviation.

Only five years later, Sikorsky would find himself in the United States, beginning a second illustrious career that would contribute first the famous Clipper transoceanic planes and then the most widely used aircraft in U.S. aviation history — the helicopter.

Igor was born into an intellectual Kiev family. His father encouraged his children — Igor had two sisters and a brother — to read, think, talk and argue, to be creative.

Young Igor was a Jules Verne fan. He became enraptured with Verne's *Clipper of the Clouds*, in which the great French author preached the gospel of the *Albatross*, an extraordinary flying machine. It could rise and descend vertically, hover and maneuver. The *Albatross* was, in short, a modern helicopter, and Verne's book persuaded Igor Sikorsky to build one someday.

But first, like so many aviation pioneers, he dabbled in motorcycles, building himself a steam-powered model. In 1909, he designed and built a couple of helicopters that didn't work, then some small "pusher" planes with rear-mounted engines that did. He designated them S-1, S-2, S-3 and so on, learning from each one, improving. He was nearly alone in his career and caught the eye of various influential people — one of them the air-minded Tsar Nicholas II.

When young Sikorsky was offered the chance to head up a new aviation branch of the old Russo-Baltic Wagon Company, he went for it. He moved to St. Petersburg and in his job continued designing his "S" planes. Some were capable of conversion to warfare, for in those uneasy years, war was on everyone's mind. Igor was also free to try his hand at a multiengine plane, one that would be capable of carrying passengers or perhaps bombs.

His first monster, called the Grand, had four 100-horsepower engines and an 88-foot wingspan. The 65-foot fuselage resembled a slender speedboat, its bow rounded, its cabin tall, with glass windows like those of a deckhouse.

No one seems to have thought the Grand would fly. Locals dubbed it the "Petersburg Duck."

But on a late May evening in 1913, Sikorsky ran up the engines and took the Grand up in smooth air. He circled the field a few times, tried the effect of three engines, then brought it in gently —the largest plane ever to fly, though few aviation buffs knew it.

Igor perfected the machine, proudly led the Tsar through it, took passengers up, kept it in the air for nearly two hours — and then lost it when an engine broke loose from a plane flying above and, unbelievably, tumbled right through one of the Grand's wings.

Work started immediately on a bigger and better plane, the Il'ya Muromets. This behemoth, with about a 100-foot wingspan, finally caught the world's attention. In early 1914, when almost all airplanes had only one engine and room for only two people on a short hop, the new aircraft rumbled aloft with 16 passengers and the pilot's dog. With eight passengers, Igor smashed the Grand's world endurance record. With a crew of three, he flew the Il'ya Muromets (named for a hero in Russian history) 1,200 miles from St. Petersburg to Kiev and back, with a refueling stop each way.

They had a few adventures on that trip: For example, an engine broke an oil line and caught fire, and two of the

Issued:
June 23, 1988
Stratford, CT

crew walked out on the lower wing and beat it out with their coats. Then storm turbulence threw them into a spin that Sikorsky managed to conquer, even though it was his first one. But when things went right the men flew in great comfort, their cabin heated by the exhaust pipes, its big windows offering a splendid view during dinner. There was a bed for the weary. And those who craved a breath of fresh air could stroll on that windy observation platform.

The flight was a triumph for the young aircraft designer. And when the Great War, or World War I, broke out in August of that year, the Tsar agreed to the formation of a squadron of "Murometsy" for observation and bombing. Igor went to work.

In 1910, Sikorsky shows off his first aircraft, a simple, well-engineered biplane called S-1. So began a line of "S" planes leading to his Clippers of the 1930s.

With several machine guns and a load of bombs, the Russian plane provided a foretaste of World War II's Flying Fortress. It bombed effectively behind enemy lines and brought back superb photo coverage of German positions. When intercepted by fighters, it fought back furiously. Attacked by four German planes, one Il'ya Muromets specimen downed three and drove off the last. It lost one engine.

Sikorsky built more than 70 of the great bombers, and the wartime loss totaled only three — only one in combat, which itself gunned down three of the seven fighters that attacked it.

But the Russian Revolution ended this phase of Sikorsky's career. He fled to Paris, then in 1919 came to the United States. The U.S. Air Service knew a little of his reputation and liked the designs he offered, but this was a euphoric time of disarmament and no funds were available for a bomber.

After many false starts, Igor found financial backing, mostly from fellow Russians, and began building planes. The Sikorsky Aero Engineering Corp.

went into business on a Long Island chicken farm belonging to an old friend, Victor Utgoff, a former naval officer for the Tsar.

The S-29-A (for America) a 14-passenger transport, took shape in the Utgoff's chicken coop out of scraps of hospital bedsteads salvaged from a nearby dump. Aluminum went over the

Sikorsky (above) tries his VS-300A of 1941, an improvement — with an enclosed cockpit — on his first successful helicopter of two years before. Typically pensive (below), he combined vision with technical skill.

iron-strong framework. Rivets were so precious that when an Utgoff chicken mistook one for a pebble and swallowed it, workers and family went after the bird, retrieved the rivet first, then had a chicken dinner.

One of the Utgoff family still remembers Sikorsky as he was back in those days — a picture of Old World formality and courtesy. He showed great interest in the world's mysteries, and studied the stars with a telescope.

Thanks to a generous donation of $5,000 from composer Sergei Rachmaninoff, a fellow emigré, Sikorsky's company moved to nearby Roosevelt Field, completing the first American "S" plane in a leaky hangar. The finished aircraft was a beauty and attracted much attention, both to itself and to its designer. But nobody would buy it. The idea of a passenger plane was still too radical to sell.

Igor's company, reorganized as Sikorsky Manufacturing Corp., survived on orders for single-engine planes. But given the chance, he returned to the multiengine designs that he had pioneered. In the mid-'20s he came up with a twin-engine amphibian, the S-34. Its fuselage was essentially a boat, big enough for seven passengers. It crashed and sank on a test flight — everyone got out unhurt — but the design stayed with Sikorsky and became a trademark.

The 16-passenger S-35 was next. It was redesigned on orders of René Fonck, leading Allied ace of World War I, so he could try for the $25,000 Orteig Prize. This was offered in 1926 for the first nonstop flight between New York and Paris. Sikorsky made the modifications — adding a third engine and fuel tanks in the cabin — but Fonck's promoters cut short the neces-

Charles Lindbergh won the Orteig Prize with his epochal flight eight months later, so Fonck never made a second try. But Sikorsky benefited from the interest in international flights that Lindbergh inspired. Igor returned to his amphibian, with boat-shaped fuselages, sold many, and then designed the S-38.

This sweet, 10-place amphibian, with two 420-H.P. Wasps to boot it along at 100 miles per hour, caught the fancy of many aviation notables. The Lindberghs used it on a much-publicized Caribbean trip. African explorers Martin and Osa Johnson employed it, painting it in zebra stripes. Pan Am bought 38 of them. Other airlines followed suit. So did the Army and Navy.

The Sikorsky plant resettled in Stratford, Connecticut, where the mouth of the Housatonic River allowed testing of flying boats. It was from here that the great Clippers of the 1930s

But when his elegant Clippers started losing out to new Boeings and Martins, and United was ready to close them out, Sikorsky proposed that he now turn to helicopters. The old boyhood dream was still alive in the Russian.

The problems of vertical flight are manifold. An engine powerful enough to spin rotors that will lift a dead weight produces immense torque — the aircraft tries to turn the other way. Once that is controlled, how do you make the thing go forward, or back, or sideways?

Much work on these questions had been going on in Europe. Sikorsky gathered all the information and set to work with his test stand in 1938, measuring the various forces involved. He defeated torque with a small vertical rotor that counteracted the movement of the aircraft's tail.

In September of 1939, Sikorsky started up the Lycoming engine of the VS-300, a small framework of steel shafts and tie rods. The main rotor, its three blades built like small airplane wings, slowly began to turn. Seated under the main rotor, Igor let it gather speed, felt the tremble of the frame, then moved the controls and rose a foot or two into the air. He hovered for a moment, then came back down. He knew the strange machine would work.

Much perfecting and many modifications followed. Then came an Army contract for a single two-place helicopter. In April of 1941, Sikorsky stayed aloft for more than an hour. Next month he broke his own record. The whole concept of human flight had taken an enormous step.

The helicopter is now the most commonly used working aircraft we know. We hear it every day, bringing patients to a hospital, passengers to an airport, cargos downtown. It can haul logs out of the forest, construction beams to the top of skyscrapers. It can make rescues in all kinds of terrain. Only a farsighted genius could have designed it.

In 1972, during a meeting of the American Helicopter Society, a note was brought to the chairman. He read it and then asked for a moment of silence. Igor Sikorsky, godfather of vertical flight, had died. ■

Famed 1914 photo (see also page 38) shows Tsar's officers on open-air deck of Sikorsky's giant Il'ya Muromets.

sary tests and no takeoffs were tried with a full load of fuel.

Sikorsky wanted to delay Fonck's flight, but at dawn September 20, 1926, the S-35 with its crew of four started to roll. Unluckily, the wind had shifted moments before and the takeoff was downwind. The plane never got off the ground. It crumpled into a ditch and burned. Fonck and his mechanic got out. The other two died.

came. The three S-40s became the *American Clipper*, *Caribbean Clipper* and *Southern Clipper*, all flying to South and Central America for Pan Am and gaining matchless publicity by starring along with Fred Astaire and Ginger Rogers in *Flying Down to Rio*.

The S-42, with four engines set into a 118-foot "parasol" wing, flew nonstop to Hawaii in 1935, opening the door to Pacific air service for Pan Am. The designer seemed to have hit full stride; his company was now the Sikorsky branch of United Aircraft Corp.

CLYDE PANGBORN & HUGH HERNDON JR.

It's surprising that Fred Verville did so much for aviation without ever flying a plane. It's perhaps more astonishing that aviation also benefited hugely from a man who did nothing but fly — Clyde Pangborn. No back rooms for Clyde, no engineering formulas. His knowledge of aircraft — and it was vast — came from the gut feelings acquired in thousands of hours in the cockpit.

Clyde Pangborn came out of the mountains and forests of Idaho, a tough youngster who'd worked as a logger and miner, then — like thousands of other youths in 1917 — stormed into a recruiting office to see if he could fly for the Army. Unlike thousands of others, he made the grade.

"Upside-Down" Pangborn, who was to become one of the world's greatest aerial showmen, came out of the postwar flying boom starting in 1919. He'd never made it to France. But he knew exactly what to do with his life and before he was through dazzling crowds of thousands, he and Hugh Herndon Jr. would stun the world in 1931 by making the first transpacific flight, from Japan to America.

Hugh Herndon, left, and Clyde Pangborn, looking glum, prepare to take off in Miss Veedol, *their Bellanca monoplane, after a stop on their 1931 world flight. Clyde obviously realizes that their chances of setting a world record are slim.*

When Pangborne finished his World War I service, Army surplus planes — mostly Curtiss JN trainers, called Jennys — were a dime a dozen. Pang and an Army buddy were soon flying them over dozens of small towns along the West Coast, getting attention by looping, rolling, flying down Main Street just above the telephone wires, then landing in a meadow and waiting for the townsfolk to ride out in their buggies and Model Ts for a look.

They'd take the townsfolk up — 10 bucks a ride. They'd sleep in a barn or camp under a wing. Pretty soon they'd move on to another town. "Barnstorming," it was called, and no one realized that it was important, that the brotherhood of nomadic pilots and stuntmen in flaring jodhpurs and riding boots, heads adorned with helmets and goggles, was spreading the word that airplanes were here to stay.

Pangborn was a whiz. He could loop anything and he could walk a stick-and-fabric wing like a cat, though the thundering slipstream tugged at him. Of course accidents sometimes happened, but Clyde was bright enough to avoid the worst and strong enough to save himself when he had to.

There was that harrowing time in San Diego. He was leaping from a speeding car to a ladder slung from a low-flying plane — an old stunt, but a good one. This time everything went haywire. The speeds didn't match, the distances weren't right, and Pangborn flew off the ladder at 60 miles per hour.

Fortunately, they were over a beach so he hit sand, and when the bouncing and rolling were over, he was still in one piece. As soon as he felt up to it, he climbed on the wing of a Jenny over Agua Caliente race track and hung from the wing skid. The act spooked the horses but caught the attention of the crowd, all right. Dozens showed up to look at the plane, and many got talked into a ride.

Joining with Ivan Gates, self-styled "P.T. Barnum of Aviation," Clyde became chief pilot and partner of the largest and most successful American flying circus.

Gates' press releases glamorized the planes that flew for him and turned jaded pilots and the grease monkeys who often did the wing-walking into knights of the air and nerveless daredevils.

Clyde flew the parachute jumpers and stuntmen like "Wes" aloft to put on their acts. Wes would pretend to fall from a wing, then be jerked up short by a rope tied to an ankle. Once he pedaled a bike across the top wing. Sometimes Pang would kill his engine and glide silently downward, and Wes would scramble atop the hot cowling, then lean forward to spin the prop and restart it. He was killed, finally, when a parachute jump went wrong. It seems they all were killed, one way or another.

Gates got mad when they perished. It was an expensive nuisance to reprint his advertising posters, replacing one name with another. Pangborn suggested they come up with a generic name — something any stunt man could use.

So they decided on the Great Diavalo. From then on, it was always the Great Diavalo who kept drawing the crowds.

The Gates Circus prospered, especially after establishing a headquarters of sorts in Denver. Gates worked out a deal to advertise Texaco on the circus planes in return for full fuel tanks.

By the time Lindbergh made his flight from New York to Paris in 1927, 11 planes were wearing Texaco's "Firechief Red." Nearly a score of pilots — the number changed as the mood to move on struck — flew under Pangborn's leadership. Interest in flight boomed and the money rolled in. Even Pang, a financial innocent, banked a suitcase crammed with $25,000.

But government regulations were beginning to restrict the hell-for-leather barnstormers, and insurance rates were high because accidents had thinned the ranks of the daredevils.

Trouble was, most planes were now cabin jobs. Passengers could sit in comfort without ruining their hairdos. And small airfields had sprung up in hundreds of country towns. Flying was getting to be old stuff.

Issued: January 2, 1981, Wenatchee, WA

First Transpacific Flight · 1931

Sabishiro Beach, Japan to Wenatchee, Washington

Clyde Pangborn & Hugh Herndon Jr.

USAirmail

© USPS 1980

With her big 420-H.P. Wasp radial sticking out like a bulbous nose, Miss Veedol *cruises with Pang and Hughie near Roosevelt Field (now gone) on the bucolic Long Island of 1931. Here they took off, July 28, on their hair-raising, 'round-the-world flight.*

The best chance for an old-timer was to take a shot at a record flight. Around the world in 8 days, instead of Jules Verne's 80 — that would win prizes and glory, maybe even the lasting fame that Charles Lindbergh had achieved by flying across the Atlantic in 1927. Clyde sprang the idea on his latest barnstorming partner, Hugh Herndon Jr. He'd become a pretty fair pilot, and, more important, a badly needed source of funds.

Herndon's mother delivered the backing. Pangborn bought a Bellanca Skyrocket, a beautiful, high-wing cabin monoplane capable of lifting a lot of weight with its big Wasp radial engine. He planned carefully: across the Atlantic from New York by the ship lanes, then across Russia and Siberia to the Kamchatka Peninsula, and so across to Alaska and on to New York. Herndon would navigate, and take the controls when the going was good. With the versatile Bellanca, named *Miss Veedol*, it would be a piece of cake.

Then word reached Pangborn that Wiley Post and Harold Gatty, two topnotch pilots in a fast Lockheed, had gone around the world in a little more than eight-and-a-half days.

Pangborn and Herndon had a tough mark to shoot at. It also turned out that Herndon had gotten married — a step that Pangborn had assiduously avoided for years — and was moping about leaving his bride when takeoff time arrived in July 1931.

On her second try, *Miss Veedol* made it off the runway at Roosevelt Field, Long Island, and immediately ran into the fog they'd hoped to avoid. Once above it, on course, the exhausted Pangborn turned the controls over to the lovesick Herndon and dozed off. When he awoke, they were 10 degrees off course.

That small error could be corrected, but it was an indication of the way that the entire trip would go.

In London, Hughie was whisked away for a party and was six hours late returning to his seething partner. Bad weather over Russia's Ural Mountains slowed them. During another much-needed Pangborn nap, Hughie strayed off course again. When they landed in Siberia they got mired. Finally, they realized they were an irretrievable 27 hours behind Post and Gatty.

Pangborn thought of an alternative goal. A Japanese newspaper had offered $25,000 for the first nonstop flight from Japan to the States. He made arrangements, altered the course, and the pair flew to Japan — where they were arrested for spying. After much negotiating, *Miss Veedol* was released and topped off with gasoline until it had, noted Pangborn, "the heaviest wing loading we had ever attempted in the Bellanca." To ease things, he devised a way to jettison the landing gear and so increase speed and range. To land, they would belly in on a steel skid.

Long after they finally took off, Pangborn carefully dropped the gear. Two struts failed to come loose. "It was so cold," Pangborn wrote, "the water in our canteens, and even our hot tea, froze." The plane began to ice up. When they broke out at 14,000 feet, he turned the controls over to Hugh and performed one of his last stunts. Climbing onto the wing strut in that savagely cold slipstream, he freed the stuck landing gear assembly. It was the most perilous wing-walk of them all.

Twice during that flight, Herndon forgot to pump fuel from tank to tank. The second time, the engine quit and Pang had to dive to get the prop windmilling so he could restart. Then he tried again to snatch some sleep. "When you see city lights," he told Herndon, "it'll be Vancouver. Wake me."

Little Wenatchee's big day came when the world flyers bellied in with their wheelless Bellanca to end the first nonstop flight from Japan. Pangborn knew the Washington town: His mother lived there, and watched him land.

Hughie managed to miss the lights. Awake, Pang realized he'd even passed Seattle, so he settled on a landing at Wenatchee in the middle of Washington State. He knew the place: His mother lived there. She was, in fact, at the airdrome when her son made his usual immaculate landing — this time without benefit of wheels.

Pangborn got barely a tenth of the $25,000. In his usual way, he'd signed some preflight papers without reading them, and Hughie owned most of the prize, plus *Miss Veedol*. He'd apparently considered Clyde simply a hired pilot. Herndon did, eventually, become a competent pilot and flew for TWA. He died in 1950 after a stroke.

Short of funds again, Pangborn took flying jobs where he could until 1934, when an Australian millionaire set up an air race from an English airdrome to Melbourne.

Missing a plane's dangling ladder as he jumps from a speeding car, "Upside-Down" Pangborn goes head-over-heels, tumbling onto a beach near San Diego in 1920. In 1931 (below), "Pang," at right, gets a more dignified ride with Herndon in a flag-draped car as Wenatchee turns out a joyous parade on short notice. Their feat led to transpacific airmail service in 1935, an anniversary noted on a 1985 U.S. airmail issue (left).

The colorful "Colonel" Roscoe Turner, with self-designed uniform and waxed moustache, had entered with a new Boeing 247 — first American low-winged, twin-engine, all-metal transport. Pangborn gladly joined him.

They had their share of adventures, lost over India because heat lightning looked like the beacon they were seeking. But with the supercharged Wasp engines "Nip" and "Tuck," they finished second in the speed category and third overall. The plane, a breakthrough in design, is on display at the Smithsonian's National Air and Space Museum in Washington, DC.

Pangborn, more battered after those years of barnstorming than that Boeing ever was, finally gave in to romance. He wedded a lovely French actress just as World War II approached. The marriage lasted a year. Pang was put to work organizing the Ferry Command of the Royal Air Force and flying aircraft to Britain. Divorce was inevitable. With Pangborn, it was first things first.

He died in 1958. By then, aviation was a common form of transportation. Today, uncountable millions fly as a matter of course.

It's said that Upside-Down Pangborn took up 100,000 people himself during those old helmet-and-goggles days. That was how the popularity of flight started. That was what the barnstormers added to the story of aviation. ∎

WILEY POST

A popular Clyde Pangborn stunt was to do loops and barrel rolls at night with fireworks blazing away all over his airplane. It was a great spectacle, but a real oldie. An earlier practitioner, Art Smith, flying a Curtiss Pusher, did the same thing back in 1913 at the Oklahoma state fair. And a 15-year-old farm boy named Wiley Post watched Smith's display and decided then and there that flying was for him.

He couldn't know it then, but Post would go on to astonish the world by making two record-setting, around-the-globe flights — one solo — before tragedy overtook him.

Wiley's big family had moved from Texas to farm Oklahoma's deep soil, long before Dust Bowl days, when the corn really grew "high as an elephant's eye." But farming wasn't Wiley's dish. To get closer to aviation, he read and studied, took an auto mechanics course, and after the United States entered World War I, enlisted in the Army to study radio.

At war's end, young Wiley found work in the suddenly thriving Oklahoma oil business. Wages for a roughneck on an oil rig were high, and he saved enough to get his first plane ride with a barnstormer. Wiley loved it and realized that this godlike pilot was just a normal young man — like him. Maybe someday....

His chance came in 1924. A barnstorming "circus" flew onto a field near his oil rig. When he went over to see the fun, he learned that the parachute jumper was hurt. "Hell, I'll jump for you," said Post.

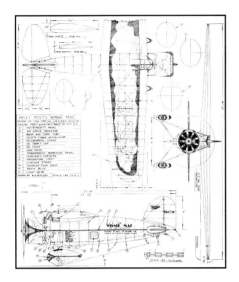

The circus took him up on it. Pretty soon he was 2,000 feet in the air, staggering out on the wing of a Jenny, his chute pack lashed to a strut. He let the slipstream blow him off the wing, hung for a moment on his safety line until he remembered to release it, then dropped, tugging the parachute free. "All motion stopped. I seemed to be floating in the air. The plane was gone.... With a sharp jerk, the parachute opened," he recalled.

He landed in a ploughed field, scraping his nose, then went on to make 99 jumps. He finally got $200 a jump and picked up flying time as the troupe traveled. But learning was so costly that he returned to the oilfields to earn the price of a plane of his own.

On his first day at a rig, another roughneck, pounding a bolt into place, sent an iron chip into Post's left eye. No one could get it out and it festered. The infection spread to the other eye and he began to go blind. His best hope was to have that left eye removed. "Take it out," he told the doctor.

The right eye came back to normal but Wiley knew that chances of becoming a pilot with only one eye weren't good. He began training himself to judge distance with one eye. "I'd practice gauging depth on hills and trees. Then I would step off the distance."

After a couple of months, he found himself more accurate than he'd ever been. He later admitted, however, that "if they ever changed the height of a phone pole or a two-story building, I'd be in trouble."

The accident paid off for him in workmen's compensation. He collected $1,800. He spent $200 of it on a damaged Canuck — the Canadian version of the Jenny — and another $340 to pay for its repairs. Suddenly he was flying.

With another Canuck owner he barnstormed, selling rides and instructing would-be pilots. And he began taking some of the oilmen he knew on business flights.

This moved Post out of the ranks of the roughnecks. He became company pilot for Briscoe and Hall, pioneers in deep drilling, and flew them to distant sites in their plane. He needed a license and got one on probation: He had to rack up several hundred hours of flight time to convince the government that he could fly with one eye.

F.C. Hall was an aviation nut and was soon anxious to buy a new cabin plane so he could take his family along in comfort. He sent Post to California to pick up a Lockheed Vega and named it after his daughter, Winnie Mae. The plane was fine but the oil business wasn't. The stock market had crashed and Hall had to sell the Vega.

Post and Gatty — household names in the summer of 1931. One-eyed Wiley Post (on right above, and opposite) and navigator Harold Gatty flew Winnie Mae *around the world in a little more than eight days, then Post did it solo — quite a feat for an Oklahoma oil rig "roughneck." The plane, a modified Lockheed Vega (detailed in diagrams above left) is now in the Smithsonian.*

***Issued:
November 20, 1979
Oklahoma City, OK***

47

Wiley flew it back to Lockheed and then landed a job there, testing and selling planes.

In 1930 he got a long-distance call from Hall: The oil business was better; get a new-model Vega and come on back to Oklahoma as company pilot.

The new plane had a 420-horse-power Pratt & Whitney Wasp engine. It could cruise at 150 miles per hour and wind up to 190 top speed. It had a seven-place cabin in its laminated ply-wood fuselage. Post flew it to Hall, then asked if he might enter a Los Angeles-to-Chicago race scheduled for that summer. Hall approved. Wiley flew back to Lockheed to get the engine beefed up to 500 H.P. with a better supercharger and to fit extra fuel tanks in the cabin.

He won the race to Chicago by better than half an hour even though his compass went on the fritz and cost him 40 minutes. Hall was delighted with the success (and publicity) gained by his new *Winnie Mae*, and agreed to Post's next idea — a fastest-ever flight around the world.

Others had made this flight, starting with two of four U.S. Army planes specially built by Douglas in 1924. These World Cruisers had taken six months. In 1929, the German dirigible *Graf Zeppelin* made the journey effort-lessly in 21 days, carrying 20 passen-gers. Wiley knew he couldn't match the luxury but thought he should be able to beat the time.

He needed a navigator and he al-ready knew the person, a transplanted Australian named Harold Gatty who ran a school for aeronautical navigation in Los Angeles. He'd laid out the route for Post's cross-country flight, and the two got along well.

While Gatty planned the course and sent for needed landing permits, Post built a navigator's station in *Winnie Mae*, aft of the cabin tanks, with an overhead hatch for sightings. The navigator's driftspeed indicator was fitted through the fuselage. Post also installed the new Sperry gyroscopic instruments for blind flying. And he trained himself to sit for hours and sleep irregularly.

They flew to Roosevelt Field, Long Island, in late May 1931, waited a month for decent weather, and were off on June 23 at the crack of dawn. The idea was to refuel in Newfoundland, then fly nonstop to Berlin. Early in the flight, Gatty gave a time of arrival over Woonsocket, Rhode Island, and was correct to the second. After that, Post followed Gatty's courses rigidly. If only the rest of the trip had been that easy.

After Newfoundland, the weather over the Atlantic offered such poor visibility that Post went on instruments for hours while Gatty, unable to get a navigational fix, dozed. When the clouds broke up and Post spotted land, he put down at a nearby airfield to check where they were. It was a Royal Air Force base. "England, Scotland, or Wales?" asked Post of a mechanic.

"England, mate," said the airman.

On over Europe, weather forced Post back on instruments. Desperately tired, he and Gatty landed at Hanover, Germany, took off, forgetting to check their tanks, turned back to refuel, and finally flew on to Berlin.

Certain that strong winds at high altitudes — now called the jet stream — would boost speed records, Post designed a way to get up there and stay alive: a space suit (left), granddaddy of those worn by astronauts. It took B.F. Goodrich three tries to meet specifications. In it, Wiley probably reached an incredible 50,000 feet.

Staggering with fatigue, they still had to say all the right things to the greeters who had waited for hours.

So went the rest of the flight: Generally foul weather forced them into instrument or low-level flying. Hospitable people kept them from getting needed sleep. They flew a weary 17-hour leg across the Sea of Okhotsk, the Kamchatka Peninsula and the Bering Sea to land on an Alaskan beach near Nome. Taxiing for takeoff, the Vega hit soft sand and bent a propeller blade. Post hammered it out on a round stone and it got them to Fairbanks, where they replaced it.

They flew through a downpour to Edmonton in Canada and found the field too flooded for takeoff. So they towed the plane to Portage Avenue, had the overhead wires removed, and roared off as "electric light poles clipped by the wingtips." One refueling stop at Cleveland and they were back, circling Roosevelt Field, slipping in, wheels barely touching, before a huge crowd swamped them.

Post was praised but he was strangely unmoved. "We didn't advance the mechanics of aviation one inch," he said. Noting that some people felt he was a brainless bumpkin, carried along by Gatty's meticulous planning and precise navigation, he decided to repeat the trip solo. He needed credibility.

In July 1933, he was off again, alone, in a revitalized *Winnie Mae* now boasting a radio direction finder (RDF) and a Sperry automatic pilot. He wanted to make only five stops. First, Berlin: He became the first pilot to make it nonstop from New York. Next was to be Novosibirsk, in the heart of the old Soviet Union, but lack of sleep was getting to him — he forgot some maps and had to turn back for them. Then the autopilot, "Mechanical Mike," acted up and he paused in Moscow to get it fixed. Yet he reached his eastern Siberia stop, Khabarovsk, in good time.

Over Alaska, fatigue struck again. Lost trying to find Fairbanks, he landed at a mining town, got mired for a while, then made it to Edmonton by using the RDF. The autopilot took him toward New York and he let himself doze, holding a wrench which was tied to a finger so it would yank him awake if he slept so hard he let it fall.

Thousands waited for Post at Floyd Bennett Field. He'd knocked some 21 hours off the flight time he'd posted with Gatty. Post, said the *New York Times*, had ushered in "a new stage of long-distance aviation" by use of those new flight instruments.

Wiley had a theory that high-altitude flight could benefit from very fast westerly tail winds — what we now know as the jet stream. But pilots couldn't survive that far up with existing oxygen equipment.

A pressurized plane would be the best answer for flights at 30,000 feet. But the wooden *Winnie Mae* could never be pressurized. So Post designed a pressure suit — it featured airtight fabric and a helmet like a diver's. The B.F. Goodrich Tire & Rubber Company made it for him. He tested it at 40,000 feet and then decided to try to set a new speed record across the United States.

Assorted gremlins kept Post from setting that record. *Winnie Mae* was old and had been used hard. Even so, Post reached 48,000 feet — probably 50,000 on a flight when his barograph failed — and found the jet stream. He rode it to a ground speed of 340 mph.

Will Rogers, America's beloved humorist, had made friends with fellow Oklahoman Wiley Post, and in the summer of 1935 he persuaded Post to fly him to Alaska: He needed material for his popular syndicated column. Post had turned *Winnie Mae* over to the Smithsonian Institution (where it is now in the National Air and Space Museum in Washington, DC) and had bought a hybrid plane built from two Lockheed models. To do the Alaska trip, he ordered pontoons but couldn't get them in time. So he used those from a larger plane.

Those pontoons were weighty and made the plane nose-heavy. After the takeoff from a lake near Point Barrow, the engine quit and the plane nosed down abruptly. It slammed into the lake, killing both Will Rogers and Wiley Post, two of America's favorite people, both generous contributors to the culture and the technical achievements of the nation. ∎

WILLIAM T. PIPER

This story is really more about an airplane than a person. It was a plane so well-known before World War II that its name — Cub — became generic; any small, light monoplane was apt to be called a Cub.

Those who were a little more precise called it a Piper Cub. They may not have known just what "Piper" referred to, but the two words seemed to go together. That fact was not lost on William T. Piper. He wanted that human reaction.

The reason that the Piper Cub became almost as famous as Charles Lindbergh's *Spirit of St. Louis* was that this ubiquitous little yellow plane, so often seen circling every American town with an airport, came closer to being our "flying flivver" than any other aircraft.

If we yearned to fly, back in the '30s, and as teenagers begged a few bucks for a lesson, it was probably a Piper Cub that we clambered into.

We had barely time to sniff the glorious essence of gasoline and banana oil — the smell of wing dope —before we were off with a modest bark of 37 horsepower, lifting from the local field, looking down from the open sides of the fuselage at the grass of the meadow, the tops of trees, the houses of friends, the highway with cars going a bit faster than we were.

We took the controls when the man in back tapped us on the shoulder. Let's see — press with the left foot and push the stick to the left. There we go, a nice gentle turn — slipping and skidding a bit — to the left. Now straighten out. Try one to the right. Oops, better climb back to 1,200 feet.... And so on, until the prepaid time was used up.

Then we felt out the instructor's landing, the corrections for buffeting above the summer-warm field, the slowing, settling, holding off, the rumble of the wheels on the turf.

That was the Cub in its heyday — simple, cheap, fun. One flight and we were likely hooked. What we didn't know was the drama behind this unassuming little flying machine. For it was conceived and built by people of strong and contentious character and deeply affected by the world around it during its life span.

It was 1926 — the middle of the Roaring Twenties — when C.G. Taylor designed a small monoplane for two people sitting side-by-side.

He called it the Chummy and priced it at $4,000, relatively cheap for a new plane, but about 13 times the cost of a Model T Ford, popularly known as a "flivver." It was a good little plane because C.G. was a good designer, but he needed financial backing.

Taylor's workshop was in Bradford, Pennsylvania, once an important oil town — drilling went on around it even in the '20s. But business was slack, so an oilman named William T. Piper allowed himself to get talked into investing in Taylor's plant.

Piper was a big, rather messy man, a mixture of hardheaded business sense and airy idealism. He gave an impression of easy relaxation which belied long hours of difficult and devoted effort. He wore a ludicrously decrepit felt hat. While driving his nondescript car he ate peanuts endlessly, chucking the shells on the floor. He didn't know what pretension was. Yet everyone called him "Mr. Piper."

Issued:
May 17, 1991
Denver, CO

50

Piper persuaded Taylor to design that elusive ideal: a plane for everyone, at an affordable price. Before the plane appeared, the Great Depression rolled over the Taylor company. Mr. Piper quickly saw that the best way of saving the firm was to declare it bankrupt, then buy it.

Using his Chummy as a starting point, Taylor cut costs and came up with a very basic monoplane: a stable wing, shock cord springs for the landing gear, a couple of engine gauges but no altimeter or airspeed indicator. You had to feel your speed, mostly by the sound of air on the tubular struts. You checked your fuel by glancing at the height of a wire — buoyed up by a cork — rising out of the fuel tank.

The first engine was a disaster — only 20 H.P. It was called a "Tiger Kitten," and people began calling the plane the Cub. A fine new Continental with 37 horses and four flat, opposing cylinders took the Tiger Kitten's place. The Cub, officially Model E-2, could carry two people in its tandem cockpit. It might just get off a football field by dodging the goalposts, landed at 35 miles per hour, and cost $1,325. In 1931, the Cub's first year and about the worst of the Depression, 22 of the planes were sold.

The little plane gradually took hold at country fields and flying clubs. Money was so short at first that when a sale was made, the buyer's check had to be cashed immediately so the engine could be paid for and installed. If the buyer agreed to act as a dealer, Mr. Piper knocked the price down by 20 percent. The staff lived more on hope than salary, and were lured by one big perk: flying lessons for $1 an hour.

New people were hired. Walt Jamouneau went to work for nothing. The only person with an aeronautical engineering degree, he pretty soon was demonstrating and selling Cubs.

What a generation gap! Slick, fast, powerful and expensive, this Piper Seneca (right) bears no family resemblance to the beloved old Cub of the 1930s (opposite). That's William T. Piper leaning against his pet product at his Bradford, Pennsylvania, plant.

Then Jamouneau made some design changes in the plane that had wide repercussions. First, they improved the Cub enormously; second, they infuriated Taylor, who started firing everyone in sight. That inspired Piper finally to buy Taylor out, on good terms. Jamouneau was made chief engineer and his Cub wore his initial. It was the famous J-2.

Cubs began to be seen everywhere. Barnstormers used them. One took off from a moving car, then landed on it. One had wheels set atop the wing so he could land inverted. The word "Cub" began to enter the language.

In March 1937, a fire destroyed the Bradford plant. Piper moved to Lock Haven, Pennsylvania, right in the middle of the state. He agreed to use a vast, empty mill that was gathering dust, but was sure his company (it would soon be called Piper Aircraft Corp.) could never fill more than one floor.

The company scrimped and suffered during the move and the rebuilding, then started growing again. Improvements to the Cub included engines from companies other than Continental. One was the Lycoming, the same engine that Igor Sikorsky, up in Connecticut, was putting on his first helicopter.

Piper publicity continued. A pilot made a long nonstop flight, refueling by plucking cans of gasoline from a fast-moving pickup truck. As World War II approached, Mr. Piper turned out some 1,800 planes in a year. His company had become the world's largest manufacturer of aircraft.

President Roosevelt asked for a Civilian Pilot Training (CPT) program so that the Army and Navy wouldn't be starved for pilots if and when war came to the United States.

No sooner had Hitler invaded Poland in September 1939 than ideas began to buzz around the light plane industry, suggesting that there was a

place for small aircraft in the military — not just training CPT pilots, but for taking the Big Brass aloft for a look at the front, carrying messages, dropping supplies, rescuing downed pilots, and above all, spotting for field artillery.

During the next year's maneuvers, big Air Corps observation planes broke down right and left as they tried to land on rock-strewn patches of flat road. So the "grasshoppers," as they were called, got another chance. Aeroncas, Pipers and Taylorcrafts —four planes of each make, piloted by civilians — did all that was asked of them and more, without problems, for free. When Pearl Harbor was blown apart in December of that year, the idea of a "Grasshopper Air Force" had already proved its worth, and the light plane industry boomed with military orders.

Painted olive drab, the little planes — mostly Pipers, now designated L-4s — wrote a war history of their own, rich with anecdotes. Though frequently fired on by American gunners who hadn't yet learned that there was such a thing as an L-4, the "grasshoppers" called in devastating artillery fire during the North African invasion and campaign, for example.

In Italy, an L-4 pilot braved low clouds and drizzle in a mountain pass to spot German artillery fire for his own guns to silence. He finally accomplished his mission but stayed far too long for his fuel supply and wound up flying blind in the mountains.

Cubs are born on the Piper assembly line (left) during their heyday. World War II changed their familiar yellow to olive drab as they joined up to spot for artillery, deliver messages, and fly the Big Brass over the lines. Gen. Dwight D. Eisenhower rides in the backseat of the Piper L-4 (above).

He let down through the clouds, found trees and rocks suddenly ahead, and a patch of muddy road where trucks were rolling. White stars were on them: Americans.

"I had merely time," he wrote, "to pull back on the stick and to slap the throttle wide open, when my left landing gear bounced off the top of a two-and-a-half-ton truck. The airplane continued to mush forward about 150 feet and settled nose-high into a muddy slope." Except for a broken prop, the plane was fine. The pilot got a skinned nose.

L-4s flew off wooden ramps on landing craft. Where there was no level ground, they used the Brodie device, a cable strung tightly between uprights. The plane hooked onto a sling that traveled on the wire. When the Cub wound up to flying speed, the pilot released his hook and flew away. To land on a Brodie, he mushed in slowly and hooked onto the sling. Brodies were sometimes hung from the gunwales of ships.

The "grasshoppers" were so effective as artillery spotters that often a commander would send one up just to make an appearance. The sight of an olive-drab Cub skittering around in the distance frequently was enough to still enemy artillery.

A few grasshoppers got lost; one got a direct hit from an American 155-mm shell on its way to a distant target. But the damage they caused the enemy, at very low cost, provides an interesting lesson in the economics of warfare. As Devon Francis has written in *Mr. Piper and His Cubs*, the definitive work on the Piper story, "A single artillery battalion could deliver fifty tons of explosive steel an hour. One tiny L-plane could and did command the fire of several battalions on one target."

The planes rescued pilots downed in jungle areas, wherever a patch could be hacked out. They straightened out traffic jams, evacuated wounded, delivered mail. Pilots learned to land where cows were grazing: That meant the field wasn't mined. One fire-eater rigged bazookas to his wing struts and reportedly knocked out five German tanks.

So the flimsy little heroes fought the Big War, and that was about the end of them. The '50s and '60s were too sophisticated for an airplane that, for a while, cost $995. Mr. Piper, with his battered hat and his peanut shells, had to face the real world. Experts came to help his company make money. It is now part of a conglomerate.

At about $1,000, the J-2 Piper Cub (above) came close to realizing the dream of a "flying flivver." Sturdy, forgiving, easy to fly and above all, fun, it remained what the legendary "Mr. Piper" (left, in his 80s) first envisioned — a trainer for beginners.

The Cub grew up. A souped-up version, the Super Cub, appeared — a fine plane for bush pilots. Then came new planes, low-winged, with tricycle landing gear and Indian names: Cherokee, Pawnee and the twin-engine Apache, Comanche, Aztec, Seneca and Navajo.

In 1969, William T. Piper died at the age of 88. Three months before his death, two young men had landed on the moon. Yet when Piper was born, Wilbur Wright was only 14, his brother Orville 10. Samuel Langley had not yet moved into the secretary's office at the Smithsonian Institution. Octave Chanute was one of the few Americans who thought much about the possibilities of human flight. He wondered about it: a flying machine for everyone. Perhaps it could happen, some day in the future.... ∎

ADDITIONAL STAMPS

For 74 years, ever since it inaugurated airmail flights, the U.S. Postal Service has issued stamps that have paid deserving tribute to aviation and its daring pioneers. Many of these directly relate to individuals honored in the USPS Pioneers of Aviation Series.

For example, when the Series was conceived, America's most famous pilot already had been honored on two stamps. Charles Lindbergh's solo flight across the Atlantic Ocean in 1927 so electrified the world that only three weeks later, he became perhaps the only living individual honored on a U.S. stamp (third row, center, at right). In 1977, 50th anniversary year of his feat, a commemorative stamp (second row, left) paid tribute to Lindbergh.

Amelia Earhart, first woman to fly the Atlantic, preceded inspiring Aviation Pioneers Blanche Stuart Scott and Harriet Quimby on a 1963 airmail stamp (third row, right).

Orville and Wilbur Wright, who "started it all" and who grace the first pair of Pioneers of Aviation Series stamps, also were honored on a 1949 airmail stamp (third row, left).

One of Aviation Pioneer Glenn Curtiss' creations, the A-1, appears on the Naval Aviation stamp issued in 1961 (second row, right).

When the USPS began airmail service to the Orient, it used China Clippers designed by Aviation Pioneer Igor Sikorsky that appear on three airmail stamps issued in 1935 and 1937 (first row, left and right, and second row, center).